Praise for *The Social Employee*

Mark and Cheryl Burgess show real-world examples of how social is fundamentally changing brands. An important read for the legions of newly minted social employees eager to jump into the fray and start making an impact.

—**Jennifer Aaker,** General Atlantic Professor of Marketing, Stanford University, and coauthor, *The Dragonfly Effect*

In today's socially connected world, companies have to leverage their internal talent in order to drive business results. *The Social Employee* will help any company become more social, relevant, and innovative.

—**Dan Schawbel,** bestselling author of *Me 2.0* and *Promote Yourself* and columnist for *TIME* and the *Wall Street Journal*

Anyone struggling to harness social media will want to read this important book. It provides a fresh perspective—focusing on empowering and motivating the "social employee" to represent the brand. Using a host of case studies, the authors explain that success involves supporting those employees with a social listening program, C-Suite commitment, communication prioritization, systems to deliver the culture of the firm, and methods to manage risk.

—**David A. Aaker,** PhD, Vice-Chairman, Prophet, and Professor Emeritus of Marketing Strategy at the Haas School of Business, University of California, Berkeley. Author of 15 books and widely recognized as the founder of the strategic branding discipline

Big brands, big changes, big stakes . . . what's not to love? For the brands tentatively dipping their toes into the social business pool, *The Social Employee* is a much-needed push into the deep end: it's time to learn to swim. This book belongs on the desk of anyone serious about learning what it means to be an employee in the new social era.

—**Mark Fidelman,** Managing Director, Evolve Capital; *Forbes* contributor; and author of *Socialized!*

The Social Employee perfectly describes the current business environment, the challenges companies face, and how the more pioneering brands are leading us to the light at the end of the tunnel. Whether you're a new hire working your way up through the corporate ranks or a C-Suite executive, you need to read this book.

—**Jacob Morgan**, author of *The Collaborative Organization*, Principal/Cofounder of Chess Media Group

The Social Employee is more than a window into how the workplace has changed. It is your must-read guide for how to unlock the power of your employees to build your brand's reputation, productivity, and profits. Buy this book to empower your leadership and employees; in fact, buy them all a copy and watch your company transform.

—**Simon Mainwaring**, *New York Times* bestselling author of *We First*

Passion. Engagement. Authenticity. *The Social Employee* shows us why these traits above all others are the key to success in the new social era. This book belongs in the collections of executives, employees, and students alike. An absolute must-read for those ready to be pioneers in a brave new era.

—**Ann Charles**, Founder & CEO, BRANDfog

It's a giant step for brands to both grasp and act upon what it truly means to be social. Mark and Cheryl have captured powerful examples of companies doing both, adding clear insights to make them actionable. *The Social Employee* demonstrates how companies that authentically connect with things that are meaningful to employees and customers reap rewards of loyalty from both.

—**Andy Smith**, coauthor, *The Dragonfly Effect*

This book is a must-read for aspiring social businesses! Companies need to teach customer-facing employees how to nurture their personal brands as they build the company brand. *The Social Employee* lays out the *why* and the *how* to empower any sized business to transform their team into a network of authentic, socially savvy brand ambassadors.

—**Jon Ferrara**, CEO, Nimble; Founder of GoldMine,
a CRM Pioneer; coauthor, *Social CRM for Dummies*

In the future, there will be two types of companies: those that monitor and stifle the social activity of their employees and those that empower the social activity of their employees. Smart organizations will be found in the second group, and this book will help you get there.

—**BJ Emerson,** coauthor of *The Tasti D-Lite Way: Social Media Marketing Lessons for Building Loyalty and a Brand Customers Crave*

If there's one thing the incredible success stories of big brands like IBM, Adobe, and Southwest Airlines show, it's that going social isn't a predetermined, paint-by-numbers process. Companies have a duty to listen to their employees and encourage them to chart the course on their social journeys. Today, corporate brands come alive through the personal brands of their people. *The Social Employee* is a fantastic testament to this, masterfully marking this watershed moment in business.

—**William Arruda,** author of *Ditch. Dare. Do!*
and *Career Distinction*

The transition from simply using social media within the business to becoming a true social business—where content sharing and social networking are integrated into processes across the organization—is an imperative yet frightening journey. Cheryl and Mark Burgess show how it's done, using examples from top global brands. *The Social Employee* is a must-read guidebook to empowering and energizing workers to build powerful brands from the inside out.

—**Tom Pick,** Digital Marketing Consultant
and Managing Editor, *Webbiquity*

THE SOCIAL EMPLOYEE

How Great Companies
Make Social Media Work

CHERYL BURGESS AND **MARK BURGESS**

New York   Chicago   San Francisco   Athens   London   Madrid

Mexico City   Milan   New Delhi   Singapore   Sydney   Toronto

1 2 3 4 5 6 7 8 9 0 QFR/QFR 1 9 8 7 6 5 4 3

ISBN   978-0-07-181641-0
MHID   0-07-181641-0

e-ISBN 978-0-07-181642-7
e-MHID 0-07-181642-9

Library of Congress Cataloging-in-Publication Data
Burgess, Cheryl.
 The social employee : how great companies make social media work / by Cheryl Burgess and Mark Burgess.
   pages cm
 ISBN 978-0-07-181641-0 (alk. paper) -- ISBN 0-07-181641-0 (alk. paper) 1. Internet marketing. 2. Branding (Marketing) 3. Social media--Economic aspects. 4. Business networks. I. Burgess, Mark.- II. Title.
 HF5415.1265.B867 2013
 658.8'72--dc23   2013008757

McGraw-Hill Education books are available at special quantity discounts to use as premiums and sales promotions or for use in corporate training programs. To contact a representative, please visit the Contact Us pages at www.mhprofessional.com.

This book is printed on acid-free paper.

The social employee is the window into the Brand's Soul.
To our amazing son Kent, and to Norma,
who inspires us with a mother's love.

Contents

FOREWORD

In an age where social media rips the covers off the behind-the-scenes aspects of business, leading brands are realizing the importance of encouraging their employees to develop social voices. Bringing a human face to institutional brands, social media can help companies communicate within their own employee bases, connect with interested customers, and cultivate other key stakeholders as never before. It is a two-edged sword, but given that it is undeniably here, now, social media must become a critical piece of a brand's arsenal—not just as a general way to connect with fans, but as a way to increase the surface area of communications throughout their rank and file, as well as with the external world.

Mark and Cheryl Burgess's premise, that social media can foster more employee dedication, productivity, and brand value, is hard to prove quantitatively, but they back it with sharp examples, and lay out the building blocks needed to make an effective strategy happen. It is not just a question of adopting an internal social platform (such as Yammer, Chatter, or others), nor is it just about encouraging key employees to blog. It requires a complete, thoughtful strategy that recognizes the barriers to getting employees engaged, acknowledges new muscles a company has to build, and realizes that the intelligence gathered from conversations is as critical an asset as the fact that employees are communicating in the first place.

It all starts with listening, and while we see many companies paying lip service to the notion, few really turn it into a deliberate part of their operations. A broad range of social tools (including McKinsey's own joint venture with Nielsen, NM Incite) are now available to parse and analyze what people are saying about a brand. These social tools generate more than just trend reports. They are the frontline warning signals of issues to immediately address or opportunities to ride. To act quickly, you have to plug the right managers into the information stream, and practice how the processes for fast action should work.

Social conversations cut across the Customer Decision Journey. Whether in the early stages of engagement, during the buying process, or as someone is using a product or service, customers can now send signals about the experience. Leaders set up war rooms where frontline employees monitor everything being said about a brand online and engage the participants when appropriate. They promote Twitter handles for customer service where reps have special protocols that let them turn around a customer's problem in the moment. Special attention is given to Facebook posts and content is found that can be reused to further build their brands. This is not low-level activity in the bowels of the company. This is critical frontline, brand-exposing interaction, and making it all work should be an executive-level priority.

As that happens, leaders quickly realize that they are creating, gathering, and reusing more content for all of these social interactions than ever before, such as direct posts on YouTube, Facebook, Twitter, Pinterest, and elsewhere by the brand's marketing department. But they also need to feed content to the employee base, give them material they can use in posts, and leverage the power of their employees' own connections to get material out. The content doesn't only come from the brand—it should be fed by posts from everyone interacting with the brand. Just as supply chain strategy has become a critical part of most companies' operations, building a Content Supply Chain is becoming a new operations priority. The growing complexity of moving content, measuring impact, optimizing, following-up, and continuously learning from it all will make Marketing Operations the next frontier for productivity improvement. The examples in this book illustrate that the right approach to social media, both inside and across a company's boundaries, can help tremendously.

Despite buying internal social media software services, most companies find it hard to establish deep engagement across their employee base. When most people live with their email window open, toggling to a separate social media stream could be seen as cumbersome.

But with a good seed base, incentives for participating, and sharing strong success stories, leaders are able to light up the value of becoming engaged and capturing great content for all to use. For frontline employees in sales and service, having a searchable database of great tips and a network of comrades to ask questions become not only a powerful source of information, but also a connection base to other employees and to the brand.

After many discussions with executives, I have found that the whole concept of social media is so fraught with risk that it becomes almost too scary a topic to address. This inevitability makes it a critical boardroom issue. It takes an enterprise, with thoughtful cultivation of employees, fast feedback processes, content supply, and an overall strategy for how to engage across the decision journey, to make it work. As Mark and Cheryl Burgess show, the right foundation can give a brand the ability to quickly spot disgruntled posts, develop an appropriate response plan, engage the writer, tap into the power of their network to get the right information out to the public, and use the whole experience to rebuild trust.

It is time to have the tough conversations about transparency. The cloak is off, and all can be revealed. Make sharing an asset. Disclose who is behind the brand, what you stand for, how you operate, and how you work together to address customers' needs. Make it your voice. Make it something that helps employees as well. Powerful networks have long been a source of competitive advantage. The time has come to build your own.

David C. Edelman
Global Co-Leader
Digital Marketing and Sales Practice
McKinsey & Company

INTRODUCTION

You never quite know where the current is going to take you.

In 2010, we founded Blue Focus Marketing with a simple purpose: to help brands focus on building profitable relationships and growing their business through social media engagement. Even at that time, social media tools for business and communication were already beginning to redefine every industry with which they came into contact. So powerful, so pervasive was social media's forward movement that it began to take on a certain amount of inevitability. Whereas a few years prior, social media presented itself simply as a possible future, by 2010 it had become increasingly apparent that it was *the* future.

Unfortunately, everywhere we looked, brands were swimming against the current, exerting tremendous amounts of energy and resources simply to stay in the same place. From a business perspective alone, this short-term strategy for survival that completely ignored the larger social trends at play seemed like an incredible waste. In the midst of a recession, this not only seemed irresponsible, but unsustainable. As anyone who has ever tried it can attest, swimming against the current is exhausting. Stay at it long enough, and every last bit of energy at your disposal will be spent. We watched as brand after brand reached its breaking point, expending all resources before surrendering to the currents, and having nothing to show for it in the end. Some brands miraculously survived the process, but far too many simply didn't.

The loss was senseless and unnecessary. It wasn't that these struggling brands didn't have solutions available to them—they did. The solution, social business, was there all along. For one reason or another, brand after brand dismissed it either as a fad or as an unworkable utopian fantasy. Of course, as the success stories in this book show, social business is neither of these things.

We're Still in the First Inning

To a certain extent, we can't fault any brand for showing reluctance to adapt. Change is scary regardless of what the circumstances are or what's at stake. When it comes to adapting an entirely new way of doing business, the stakes couldn't be higher. Even if the decision is ultimately misguided, most of us feel safer trying to stay the course and weather the storm.

In the case of adopting social business practices, it wasn't just that this new way of doing things marked a fundamental shift in the way organizations would operate, it was the fact that the course toward this new horizon was largely uncharted. If brands chose to change, they were going to have to do it independently.

Even as this is being written in early 2013, most companies still face this stark reality. Only a very small percentage of brands have dared to venture into this new world. Our interviews with several of these brands clearly revealed their successes in the new world of social business; however, all were unanimous with their opinions that a great deal of work still lay ahead. In the game of social business, we're still in the top of the first inning.

Despite this humbling realization, there's no denying progress has been made. A few years ago, no one even knew the rules to the game, let alone what it would be called. Today, it is well known that the game is called social business, and most have agreed on a basic set of fundamental principles. Now that the basic principles of the game have been set forth, it's time to play ball!

The Case for the Social Employee

This book is not an argument for social business. Many books published in the past few years have sufficiently cleared that ground.

Those works, as well as the work of countless bloggers and thought leaders, have tremendously contributed to the themes we explore in this book. Now that the case for social business has been made, it's time for us to carry the conversation forward in order to examine the primary driver of the social business—the social employee.

Just as baseball games are played by teams, those teams are comprised of individual players, each with a specialized role designed to help the team win. It's been said that the outcome of a baseball game is determined by the individual players on the team. We see the social employee's role in business in much the same way. This is not to say that winning the ball game isn't a team effort—collaboration lies at the very heart of a true team effort. For collaboration to truly ignite throughout a social business by tearing down silos and driving innovation in new and surprising ways, individuals must be empowered with the right tools and training to build lasting collaborative relationships—whether those relationships are with coworkers, managers, or customers.

So why the social employee? What makes them so different from the employees of a traditional command-and-control organization? The answer to this question can be somewhat nuanced. Like most aspects of social business, these reasons often have to be experienced to be believed. It is our sincere hope that this book will take you through that process, regardless of whether you are approaching this content as an employee, an executive, a business owner, an industry analyst, or an educator hoping to prepare the next generation for a bold new world.

The simple answer, however, is that your employees are already on the front lines of your brand. Social media has redefined the way we treat each other as individuals, the way customers interact with brands, and the way employees interact with employers. Social employees matter because they already exist—regardless of whether the organizations they work for recognize them or not. As long as social media continues to play such a prominent role in people's daily lives, social employees aren't going anywhere any time soon.

For too long, the idea of the "soulless corporation" has dominated public perceptions of major brands. Social media practices argue that this no longer has to be so. In fact, this outdated perception goes directly against a brand's best interests. Social employees are the windows into a brand's soul. They are brand ambassadors to the public, building human relationships that are beneficial not just for the business outcomes produced, but for the emotional outcomes that are encouraged as well. Social employees give a brand its *why*, a reason for existence that extends far beyond the simple notion of profitability.

Always Evolving

When AT&T engaged us to become two of the first external bloggers on their Networking Exchange Blog in late 2011, we couldn't imagine in what exciting directions this new venture would take us. At the time, we were happy enough simply to join another community of interest and expand the reach of our brand. As external experts, we were tasked with crafting blogs on social media topics in order to generate awareness of what this concept meant for business and foster social engagement. We didn't realize at the time that our involvement would help put us at the very tip of the social media iceberg.

In addition to producing these blog posts alongside a select team of AT&T employee bloggers, in February 2012, Cheryl was asked to speak at the AT&T Networking Leaders Academy Annual Conference in Bedminster, New Jersey. While there, she delivered her talk, "Expanding Your Influence: Lessons in Networking." As a result of our experience of blogging on behalf of AT&T, a seed began to grow in our minds, one centered around the concept of the social employee. Its first manifestation came in the Blue Focus Marketing post, "The Rise of the Employee Brand,"[1] and eventually sprouted and grew into the content of this book.

As social entrepreneurs, we made social business practices an essential part of our culture from the beginning. However, as was reinforced for us time and again through both our expanding role in the marketing community and in the process of writing this book, the needs of the social business are constantly evolving. While at the onset of this project we had spent a considerable amount of time expanding our networks and sharing rich content with our communities, we had never undertaken a writing project of this magnitude.

As many of our colleagues who have produced books can attest, the writing process contains a great deal of moving parts. Between coordinating interviews with representatives from several brands, communicating with our publisher, and actually writing the chapters, we knew that staying organized was essential for survival. To succeed, we had to make sure we practiced what we preached, adopting project management and organizational tools into our day-to-day operations. The adoption curve on the different platforms we utilized wasn't always smooth, but the process afforded us valuable insight into what it meant to truly operate as social employees. We consider this experience an integral component of the final product, as it taught us how exciting it could be to operate in a business environment that was constantly evolving.

Dare to Be Disruptive

So with the wind at our backs, off we sail into uncharted territory, retracing as best we can the course of the pioneers who first cleared the way for us. Until social business adoption reaches its inevitable tipping point, we understand that arguments in favor of concepts like the social employee will continue to have their detractors. Every day we see executives, managers, and employees alike continue to drag their feet, wondering when this social media fad might play itself out. So far, it appears they will have to keep waiting.

To those detractors, we thank you for joining the growing conversation surrounding social businesses and their employees—a conversation in which we are merely a small part ourselves. Further, we accept your challenge: without dissenting voices, we would have little reason to try to justify our own thinking. We write this book as much for social business detractors as for anyone else. Even if after reading this book, you are still unconvinced of the power of the social employee, it is our hope you will at least learn something about the current business climate along the way.

This hope is what drives the challenge we present in this book: dare to be disruptive. Just as it is true that all new ideas need their skeptics, it is equally true that the status quo needs to be shaken out of apathy from time to time. It is a fact of human nature that many of us hold on to certain ways of doing things long after the favored approaches have outlived all stages of usefulness. In many cases, people forget the reasons the approaches were chosen in the first place.

Disruptive thinking drives innovation. It is a reminder that the *why* should always take precedence over the *how*. Not every disruption leads to the solution that may be sought, but it will usually teach something new along the way. As the swirling sea of the business world stretches out before us, there's no denying we currently find ourselves in a state of flux. The status quo simply isn't producing results quite the way it used to.

Whether the choice is made to become involved or not, it should be remembered that no one can swim against the current forever.

PART I

Weathering a Sea Change

CHAPTER 1

The New Normal—Even Change Is Changing

The whole world has gone social.

Well, perhaps that's not entirely true. As far as the human race is concerned, the world has always been social. Humankind, after all, would not have lasted very long if early societies hadn't adapted a spirit of collaboration, common purpose, and shared destiny. We are inescapably and inextricably linked together. We rely on these connections for just about everything, from interactions as simple as checking in with loved ones to activities as complex and multifaceted as coordinating social revolutions. We can no longer ignore the fact that social media platforms have fundamentally rewired the way we build relationships in the digital village.

While going social in itself may be nothing new, the nature of the term keeps changing. Each new interpretation manages to redefine the nature of change itself. Even change is changing, it would appear, and it continues to change so rapidly that it has become the only constant in a business environment driven by its need to accurately project the present into the future.

Discarding Assumptions

A fundamental assumption of marketing over the last century has been that brands were not only able to anticipate the changes new technologies and innovations would bring, but that it was their responsibility to drive those changes. Today, save for a few of the more prescient brands, businesses are still struggling to accept the idea that social networking platforms can—and do—offer a myriad of solutions designed to increase productivity and reduce costs.

The sense of urgency surrounding the role of social media in business continues to grow. Many brands have come to accept that social media is the way of the future, yet most don't know how to take the first step in getting there. A deluge of books have appeared in the last few years to help guide businesses through this transitional period. All of these books were written by some of the most prominent thought leaders in the marketing community. They cite a wealth of research to demonstrate the ways a properly structured social business can not only bolster a company's bottom line, but also help produce a culture of engaged brand ambassadors ready to shepherd their brand's identity into the modern age.

This book benefits tremendously from the groundbreaking works of these authors. In the following chapters, we hope to add to the conversation with an in-depth exploration of what social business in practice looks like, and how these models affect employees on an individual level. We accept as fact the idea that social business is no longer just a good idea—it's the reality of the modern brand. To put it bluntly, companies risk extinction if they aren't having internal discussions about what social business might mean for their organizations as well as for their employees. The well-documented falls from grace of cherished, long-lived companies like Kodak and Hostess have demonstrated that every brand is vulnerable in the digital age.

The Social Employee: Coming to a Workplace Near You

If the stakes sound high, that's because they are! Businesses that fail to adapt will lose the race to capture the modern brand's most valuable asset, and the subject of this book: the social employee.

Many reading this book may be wondering: Why have we chosen to put so much emphasis on the social employee as an individual? Is it arrogant—perhaps even idealistic—to think that the contributions of individuals can have so much cumulative value for businesses, from the smallest start-up to the largest multinational corporation? Perhaps, but we'd like to think that we're simply observing a growing awareness in the marketplace, and putting a name to a very real phenomenon.

Our friend and expert analyst Mark Fidelman put it best when he said, "The new workforce wants, even demands, to work for a social business. If you want to hire the best talent (especially the best young talent) you must demonstrate that you *are* a social business."[1] The reality that we're seeing today is one in which the social employee and the social business is a package deal. Even in our relatively flat economy, companies are coming to the realization that today's workers expect more out of their employers than just a steady paycheck.

According to the data of recent employee interviews collected by *Forbes* in an article titled "10 Reasons Your Top Talent Will Leave You," the divide between employee and employer is reaching dangerous levels:

▸ Over 40 percent don't respect their superiors.
▸ Over 60 percent don't feel their career goals align with their current job trajectories.
▸ Perhaps most telling of all, over 70 percent don't feel appreciated or valued by their employer.[2]

These statistics don't bode well for employers. High turnover rates only consume precious time and resources—commodities that no brand can afford to waste in the current economic landscape. Of course, time and resources aren't even the greatest commodities at stake—the employee is. Companies that fail to activate their employees in the social era don't just risk losing their workers, they risk losing their *best* workers.

With this in mind, activating employees around a brand is not just a matter of employee retention, but rather a matter of unlocking an employee's hidden talents. Social business models do much more than improve culture within a brand; they bring the many and varied employee skill sets and areas of expertise to the forefront—traits essential for driving both disruptive innovation and productivity.

This kind of thinking in the social era must comprise the DNA of a brand's fundamental principles. As contradictory as it may sound, a brand must first set its sights internally in order to build trust in the marketplace and ultimately bolster its bottom line. According to Jennifer Aaker, General Atlantic professor of marketing at Stanford Graduate School of Business and coauthor of *The Dragonfly Effect*, "You're finding stronger brands are built inside out where the brand inside is so powerful, and then eventually that is disseminated to customers such that when customers hear about some brand action, it's easier to trust that brand."[3]

We call this process employee branding. The more faith a brand puts in its employees, the more willing those employees are to represent their brands in public spaces and drive profits. We asked our friend David Aaker, professor emeritus at UC Berkeley and vice chairman at Prophet, what the term *employee branding* meant to him.

> Employee branding means getting your employees to know what the brand stands for and cares about. One test is to pose these two questions to a sample of employees: (1) What does your brand stand for? and (2) Do you care? If the answers are not forthcoming, you have little chance of brand building, creating on-brand programs, and avoiding inconsistencies in customer touch points.

As social media continues to grow in complexity, no public space is more important than the digital frontier. The social employee can offer a window into a brand's soul, driving a brand's reputation to new heights through rich engagement and authentic representation. Throughout the following chapters, we will explore what this new kind of employee looks like, the conditions in which they expect to work, and the need for strong leadership to define and build a culture that enables these employees to not simply succeed, but to thrive. But in order to get there, we must first take a closer look at the current business climate in which we find ourselves.

The Paradox of Change

For brands that haven't quite put the pieces of the social jigsaw puzzle together, the unknowns inherent in change seem to be lurking around every corner, waiting to spring out and render those brands' best laid plans entirely obsolete. In a 2012 blog post, John Hagel, cochairman at the Deloitte Center for Edge Innovation, acknowledges the sometimes bewildering nature of change, but points out that even within change, people can define constants to guide them through the process. "My advice based on the experience that I have accumulated over the years: decide what isn't going to change, especially in three key domains: principles, purpose, and people."[4]

We find no small coincidence in the fact that these three domains also account for the most essential pillars for success in social business. Hagel believes these traits fuel "the passion of the explorer," acting as a north star, so to speak, as a person sets sail for unknown destinations. It's not difficult to see how Hagel's concepts of change can be applied to modern branding practices. As we explored the experiences of social employees at several leading brands, these themes cropped up continually. We believe they mark the essential difference between playing at social business and actually *being* a social business.

Hagel also stresses that, when a person sets sail under the flag of change, that person can't—and shouldn't—know their precise destination. Brands should absolutely establish the working conditions for their social journeys, but they should plan to be surprised by a series of new discoveries along the way. To Hagel, explorers have "a clear and unwavering commitment to a domain of action that defines the arena [they] intend to play and grow in. That domain will undoubtedly evolve rapidly, often experiencing disruptive change, and the boundaries of the domain are likely to change over time."[5] Applying this idea to social business, we can interpret the "arena" Hagel describes as one that arises out of a brand's mission, vision, and values—elements that must be championed by every employee in a company, from the C-Suite down to the summer intern.

It's clear that the journey toward building a business full of engaged, considerate employees cannot be made overnight. We can't know where exactly this journey will take us, but we can expect to be profoundly changed throughout the process. We asked our friend, social media guru Simon Mainwaring, how brands can expect to plot their course on the social journey:

> There is no map to follow or destination to seek other than the one companies set for themselves. They must be their own compass in a fast changing marketplace or leave themselves open to feeling overwhelmed or simply broadcasting their schizophrenia. So brands must chart a course based on their purpose, core values, and vision for what they will offer the world and bring that to life consistently across new media, channels, and marketing.

The course toward social business may not always be a clear one, but it will shape every aspect of business operations in the coming decades. As Mark Fidelman explains: "The skills needed to succeed today are not being taught in the workplace, high schools, or colleges, as they were in previous ages. Instead, they are learned through experimentation, which yields both big mistakes and stunning successes."[6]

Whether in success or failure, the consumer world is watching. The experiences consumers have are ultimately what will justify a brand's existence. The way a brand presents itself to the public reflects the way it takes care of itself internally. The social brand takes this philosophy to heart and understands that the best way to present a unified front is through impassioned individual effort.

So, before we set sail on this great adventure, it's important to understand the nature of the seas on which we'll be traveling. How exactly are brands positioned in this burgeoning social age, what challenges confront them, and what preconceptions must they shed before allowing themselves to jump into the fray and champion social employee culture (see Figure 1.1)?

Figure 1.1

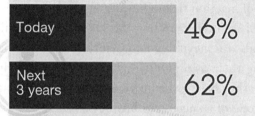

Big Social Shift

Companies are moving ahead on the social journey...

Companies increasing their investment

Today	**46%**
Next 3 years	**62%**

...but need to be better prepared for it

only 19%

have been able to measure the ROI

only 26%

are prepared to address the cultural changes

only 22%

of managers are prepared to apply social to their day-to-day work

Adopting without understanding: while more businesses continue to invest in social technologies each year, few are prepared to adopt the culture changes necessary to drive these new tools.

Credit: IBM (IBM IBV Social Business Adoption Study 2012)

Losing Control: A Brand's Greatest Fear

Throughout history, times of transition have always yielded an unfortunate by-product: fear. This is not to say that all fear is bad—expressing one's concerns is an essential part of doing business—but rather that fear's value is limited. It should inform a brand's decisions moving forward, but it should not dominate the conversation. Too much fear can prevent us from moving forward at all. When this happens, fear is no longer serving us, but rather we are serving fear. In an era where even the nature of change itself continues to change, the consequences of inaction through fear are simply too great.

Brands incapable of understanding the social era or unwilling to adapt to its demands will inevitably find that they no longer have any say in determining their own public image. They will slowly come to understand that they have lost control of their brand identities, an essential cornerstone of a successful business. Worse than the loss itself, though, is the fact that these brands won't understand how it happened.

In reality, brands lost control—or at least lost sole proprietorship—of their brand identities the moment social media platforms became integrated into our daily lives. The most innovative brands unafraid of the new social frontier willingly ceded control of their identities. They saw the writing on the wall: today's brands cocreate their images with their customers because they understand the ways social media has dramatically amplified the customer's voice. As Dion Hinchcliffe and Peter Kim say in *Social Business by Design*, "Influence and power are inexorably flowing into everyone's hands now that all individuals have access to equally powerful tools for self-expression."[7] Users can leverage social media to describe their brand experiences with their networks—both the good and the bad. And they love to share. A recent (and already frequently referenced) study by the Nielsen Company, a global leader in cutting-edge market research, found that 90 percent of consumers trust the opinions of friends in their network more than they trust any other source.[8]

No matter what, users are going to share their opinions on various brands as a natural extension of their social experience. The question is whether the brand will make itself available to be a part of these conversations or not. An absent brand has no chance of defending itself or reconciling an issue with a customer unless it ensures that it has a stable, authentic online presence.

The brand that joins in these conversations and shares in these experiences—whether good or bad—stands to gain a great deal in public esteem. In fact, the public's ultimate verdict on a brand often hinges specifically on how a brand responds to different social media scenarios. Brands have a choice to either use customer feedback constructively or ignore it and let the conversation continue without their input. In considering the latter, a brand still learning to navigate the social realm of the digital bazaar should remember that ignoring a problem doesn't make it go away, but instead makes it grow even bigger. In these types of situations, brands must be prepared to let their employees act as brand ambassadors, reaching out to customers authentically and in a spirit of goodwill.

Building a Collaborative Mindset

As Don Tapscott said in his 2012 TED Talk, "To me this is not an information age. It's an age of networked intelligence."[9] This distinction is important, because the latter aspect of Tapscott's binary encourages organic collaboration and data sharing. This mindset first took hold on the consumer end, with casual users looking for new ways to connect with their friends. It soon extended to business. Now, many brands are benefitting from practical solutions to old problems through the collaboration tools offered by both internal and external social networking platforms.

The implications for this new approach to information sharing and collaboration affect every human discipline—from the sciences to the arts—and therefore they affect every industry as well. One interesting result of this process is the new blurring of disciplines. Skilled media specialists are finding new ways to combine science with art, data with design, or business with pleasure—all in exciting, innovative ways. To see this in play, one need look no further than some of the current buzzwords swarming around today's marketing principles. Current popular thinking stipulates that the best measure of a brand is its "character," or its "authenticity," words once reserved exclusively for the creative realm. This begs the question: If brands do indeed depend on these kinds of intangibles, how do they produce the necessary results? Simple: by telling a story!

Buzzwords such as character, authenticity, and storytelling form the keystone in the arch of modern marketing. Without these elements, the entire branding effort collapses into the rushing stream of social media, swept away and forgotten in the unceasing tide of new content.

The question facing most brands at the moment is how they can effectively champion these traits without their efforts seeming forced and insincere. The last thing a brand wants to hear from a customer is that they are "trying too hard," as this often implies inauthentic engagement on the part of the brand. Despite these challenges, marketers must continue to be involved in every aspect of the consumer buying phase, and do so in a way that is neither intrusive nor disingenuous. We will be exploring the new dimensions of the customer buying phase in greater detail in Chapter 2.

Five Gateposts of Brand Culture

We had the opportunity to speak with John Kennedy, vice president of corporate marketing at IBM, about what he considers the essential best practices every brand must master in the social age. Throughout the following chapters, we will be using these foundational concepts as our springboard into the world of the social employee.

1: Develop a Social Listening Program

More companies are beginning to use social listening as a way to get a clearer understanding of what's being said in almost real time. They are using this information to supplement some of the traditional brand attribute and measurement studies many brands rely on. The companies that are farthest along in understanding the intersection between their brand and their culture and character, first start with a very robust social listening program. This is used as a window into how their audiences really feel about their brands.

2: Commitment in the C-Suite

Even if executives are aware of the data produced as a result of social listening, there needs to be a shared conviction among the C-Suite leaders that branding is not just marketing. The idea of being character-aligned to every aspect of company operations has to be something the entire C-Suite shares, because driving that kind of change extends far beyond the marketing department. There needs to be a degree of commitment among the leadership team that there is a strategy and intent that stems from the culture and character of the company. This strategy and intent will be found in every kind of interaction, from the back office to the front office, to everything in between.

3: Identify Signature Interactions

Companies need to identify where they have big gaps between interactions—for example, what a customer experiences versus what the company's character or brand is supposed to be. Companies should focus on the signature, critical interactions in their business models, and they need to get them right. Some will be outside the purview of the marketing department, such as product development, HR, or supply chain management. Brands need to identify what the gaps are, and then build systems to ensure that the customer experience is consistent with the brand's character in every single interaction.

4: Build Systems That Deliver Culture

Brands need to build systems, tools, training programs, and social business platforms that enable all employees in a company to deliver on the expectation of the character, culture, and brand. A brand's employees have expertise in a wide variety of functions. Companies need to view social media as a platform that allows each employee's expertise to be more accessible to the world. As such, most of these experts should be very active in social media. Their presence alone can be a differentiating factor for a brand.

5: Prepare for Risk

One consequence of the openness social media brings is new kinds of risks. All programs need a system in place to manage the risks of being a social business. Brand initiatives should set clear expectations in training and programs that ensure employees behave in the best possible way. Companies are always cautious about the risks associated with being transparent, so employees must clearly understand their roles, responsibilities, and expectations of conduct.

CHAPTER 2

The Blue Focus Marketing®
Social Employee
Möbius Model™

N ow that the fundamental principles of branding have been turned on their head, brands can't afford to keep carrying on with business as usual. Consumers are tired of feeling targeted, as if their only value to a brand is their demographic status. Brands enjoyed a great deal of success in the twenty-first century by targeting a specific market and then beaming their prospects a generic, one-size-fits-all advertisement. If the brands didn't get the results they were looking for, they'd simply become more persistent with their campaigns.

Today, however, we're well into the age of individuals. *TIME* magazine first heralded the dawning of this new era in 2006, when it boldly declared "You" to be its Person of the Year. This marked a turning point in marketing principles, as brands discovered they couldn't treat their customers as a mindless school of fish. The past few years have demonstrated repeatedly how loud the voice of the individual has become. Today's customers refuse to be treated as amorphous collections of data points. They expect engagement, and they expect respect. Social employees can utilize social media tools to act as authentic brand ambassadors in order to cultivate unique relationships with individuals where the end goal isn't simply a purchase action, but a dynamic exchange of ideas.

A New Model for New Times

If the marketer's relationship with the consumer has been fundamentally transformed, then it stands to reason that old models of consumer engagement no longer apply. The Attention-Interest-Desire-Action (AIDA) model has essentially dominated standard marketing practices since the acronym was first formalized by C. P. Russell in 1921 (though its basic operating principle preceded his publication). AIDA characterizes the customer purchase cycle as moving straight through a linear process of awareness, interest, desire, and action—the moment of purchase.

Even in its heyday, the AIDA model was never perfect. Since that time, marketing theory has evolved to acknowledge the cycle doesn't simply end with a purchase. What about the customer experience, word of mouth, brand loyalty, and consumer advocacy? All of these important factors in the purchasing cycle occur *after* the moment of action in the AIDA model. However, brands like Coca-Cola have understood for years that they couldn't build their businesses around the assumption that once somebody purchased their product, the brand's relationship with the customer ended. Coke may be somewhat of an obvious example, but it very clearly illustrates the way brand/consumer relationships are constantly renewed and redefined. People don't simply drink Coke, they identify with it. Social media has made fostering these sorts of relationships much easier and far more individualized. As a result, brands now have the opportunity to connect with both their customers and their employees on a much deeper level.

With social media, the post-purchase phase becomes perhaps the most crucial element of the process. As such, this could easily be considered the most important touch point for social employee/customer engagement. Customers who are happy not only with the product itself but with the *experience* they had in using the product have the potential to become a brand's greatest advocates. These customers are likely to share their experiences with hundreds—or even thousands—of potential new customers through their extended networks. By providing consumers opportunities to connect via multiple touch points, brands make it easy for consumers to reach out to them. And, when the consumer finds that real people actually monitor those social channels, the relationship between brand and customer deepens in mutually beneficial ways.

Avoiding the Linear

Today, brand value is largely derived not from the items a brand sells, but from the social employee's ability to continue to reach out to customers in the post-purchase phase. A brand's relationship to its buyers does not end with a purchase. In fact, in the social era, a brand's most important work begins *with* the purchase. Today's customer expects more than a shrink-wrapped package and a kick out the door. Customers seek identification with their brands. They want to see brands reflect personal values wherever possible and to see individuals within those brands reflect those values.

Unlike in the AIDA model, in the social era, customers are always in the process of renegotiating their relationships to products and brands. Each of us has the freedom to buy practically anything we want. We're used to being advertised to. We know the different ways a company will try to coerce us into making a purchase, and we're becoming more immune to the process every day. This abundance of choice has been liberating to the consumer who never has to settle for an inferior product simply because it's the only thing being offered. The challenge instead has been to determine which product among the myriad of offerings will satisfy a customer's needs the best. This determination is difficult to make because customers must constantly juggle different considerations in order to make a choice.

At one time, a customer's considerations were limited largely to the utility and functionality of an item. More recently, brands haven't been able to get by on the product alone. For instance, if a customer wants a tablet computer, brands like Apple, Microsoft, and Google all offer quality products. The great separator between the brands seeking to profit in the short term versus the brands seeking to position themselves for long-term success will not come through the products or services themselves, but through the relationships employee brand ambassadors establish with their customers.

For this reason, a brand's purpose—its mission, vision, and values—becomes critical for sustained success. In his book *We First*, our friend Simon Mainwaring champions a new concept of capitalism that he calls "profit with purpose":

> *Businesses, while making a profit, also have a positive impact on the world. A business that commits to purpose seeks to infuse greater meaning into the lives of all the stakeholders it touches— employees, customers, suppliers, distributors, community members, and all other parties affected by the business's presence.*
>
> *To summarize this version of capitalism in a single phrase:* Profit with purpose is mindful, contributory, and socially oriented.[1]

Brands championing purpose as their guiding principle must step out of AIDA's linear, business-as-usual model and empower their social employees to cultivate dynamic relationships with their customers at every stage of the buying cycle. Purpose should be ubiquitous, driving a brand's every exchange both internally and externally.

The Möbius Strip

In considering what a nonlinear model of customer engagement might look like, we came across the concept of the Möbius strip. This geometric shape is somewhat unique in the physical world. While the

Möbius strip appears to be a closed band like a bracelet, because of a twist in the band itself the object technically has only one side—although it appears to have two.

As confusing as this might sound, a Möbius strip is actually quite easy to create and visualize. Cut a thin strip of paper, twist it, and attach the loose ends together to close the loop. If you run your fingers across the surface area of the object, you will find that you can successfully trace both "sides" of the object without having to lift your finger, eventually arriving safely at your starting point. Such an object only seems possible in an M.C. Escher painting, but unlike many of the shapes in an Escher painting, Möbius strips are very easy to produce in the real world.

The tricky, and somewhat paradoxical, nature of the Möbius strip has led to much consternation in the mathematics community over the years. Mathematicians could build physical models of the Möbius strip easily enough, and its unique properties were understood through basic observation. However, until approximately 2007, mathematicians had been unable to build an equation that could consistently produce the proper shape regardless of the variables.[2]

We like the metaphor implied in this famous mathematical conundrum: here is an object that is easy to understand by experiencing it, but incredibly difficult to produce through attempts to quantify it. Such a riddle creates an unmistakable parallel with the nature of social employee engagement. Any brand can see the value of social collaboration once they've jumped into the fray, but it's much more challenging to try to define the precise formula for why it works.

The underlying message is this: brands waiting for some perfect formula for success before they engage in social business practices are wasting their time. The basic principles of going social have already been established—whether or not they're fully understood. The only way to really know the equation for success, however, is to dive in and start discovering what works.

How the Social Employee Fuels the Social Brand

The Möbius strip's unique properties make for a fascinating model, as a person traveling along its surface can successfully occupy any point on this multidimensional object without ever having to adjust their heading. In this model, the social employee traveling along the Möbius strip inevitably occupies different roles during the process of exchange. Sometimes they're right side up; sometimes they're upside down.

The plasticity of an individual's role in the cycle is an important concept in social business, especially when considering what it truly means to be a customer. Vala Afshar and Brad Martin, two

Figure 2.1   How the Social Employee Fuels the Social Brand

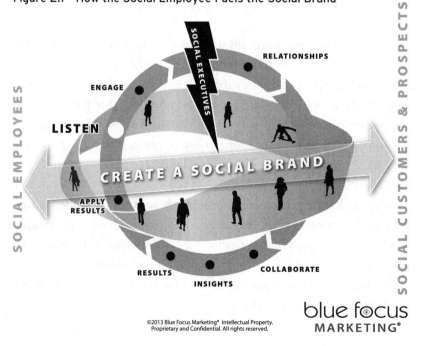

blue focus
MARKETING®

innovative social executives at Enterasys, summarized this concept very well:

> *A social business operates with the guiding principle that each employee's responsibility is to serve one another, and that those we serve, even internally, are our customers. To earn internal customer trust and loyalty, each employee must be dependable, available, responsive, and committed to the success of the whole.*[3]

In social media, brands engaged in service with purpose have a difficult time distinguishing what it means to be "customer" and what it means to be "employee." In truth, these roles are negotiable. This will be further explored in Chapter 4, but essentially, each of us behaves as employee, brand, and customer—sometimes simultaneously—throughout the course of a single day.

How the Blue Focus Marketing® Social Employee Möbius Model™ Works

The Blue Focus model includes three primary elements (see Figure 2.1):

1. Social employee
2. Social executive
3. Social customers and prospects

Social executives are responsible for communicating the overall corporate strategy to their employees. This strategy includes the brand's mission, vision, values; social media policy; and training to help guide and focus their work. Strong social leaders energize their employees, inspiring them to seek out rich social interactions. Social executives should encourage and empower employees to utilize social media channels in order to reach and engage customers and prospects. The ultimate goal of the social business is to improve efficiency, effectiveness, and customer satisfaction, as well as to add value to the social brand.

The model begins with social listening, where employees in the firm carefully monitor the market around them. Effective listening leads to a more nuanced understanding of customers, and therefore it can lead to proactive anticipation of individual customer needs. The second phase, social engagement, presents an opportunity for social employees to use various social media tools to interact more effectively with customers and prospects. This engagement organically leads to the forging of deeper customer/brand relationships.

Social employees and customers are encouraged to exchange information and to collaborate on new ideas in the pursuit of innovative ways of doing business. As the process continues, the firm gathers insights from the social employees, customers, prospects, and other stakeholders. Insights gained through these exchanges contribute to analysis of actual results versus key performance indicators (KPIs), affording the social executive opportunities to quickly understand which processes work and which do not. Finally, the model is infused with valuable learning that can be applied and reinvested in the process to enhance and strengthen the ongoing social employee/ customer relationship.

Joining the Conversation Instead of Commanding It

The success of the Blue Focus Marketing® Social Employee Möbius Model™ stems from organic, purposeful interaction. This means that traditional methods of customer engagement have to be reconsidered. We can no longer be satisfied by simply barking directives at our consumers and expecting them to leap at each new product we offer. This one-way dialogue, most commonly referred to as outbound marketing, still offers some value through traditional channels; however, it doesn't work well on the web. In the social age, these traditional approaches can't be enough; social employee engagement in the digital village, or inbound marketing, must take center stage in any serious marketing effort.

The distinction between these two approaches is very real. Brands expecting to be able to create a Facebook page and start demanding that people buy their products will likely find very low levels of engagement and conversion. Without a living, breathing human being behind that page to breathe life into the content, these marketing efforts will fall flat. Brands that simply go through the motions without empowering their social employees to champion these new outreach opportunities will have missed the point of social engagement entirely. Unfortunately, this sort of thing tends to happen to far too many brands.

In the digital village, all voices are essentially rendered equal. A brand could have tens of thousands of employees spread across the globe, but it still has to compete for precious space on a customer's newsfeed, space that won't be offered up to just anyone. Social employee brand ambassadors must first earn the consumer's trust. This will never happen if they exhaust all available social media capital on flat, aggressive sales pitches. People have never really liked being pitched to anyway; it has been tolerated because consumers felt there was no other choice. Online, people can easily block the brands lacking in social etiquette, and this ability is used indiscriminately.

Social business guru Simon Mainwaring looks at social media marketing this way: "Brands used to advertise, and then customers would respond by going out and buying the product. Now, customers are telling the brands what they want, and so the brand's first duty is to listen first and then respond with a product suggestion." To engage in social media is to join the conversation—not to start it, and certainly not to force it. It's not about the brand, it's about engagement. Joining the conversation provides benefits to current and potential consumers by offering them valuable content, activities, contests, and the like. But more than any of that, it's about having real people available for questions, supporting the consumer, and celebrating their world. As Mainwaring says, social media requires brands to shift from being the celebrity to the "primary celebrant" of a brand. The brand is not the star of the show anymore—the user is: "This is how social channels work. When the brand celebrates the customer, the customer will want to talk about that via social channels."[4]

You Can't Measure Cultural Capital

If social employees can successfully learn to engage customers by helping contribute to a culture of collaborative celebration, then those employees will reap the rewards in goodwill, viral exposure, and cultural capital. In the digital/social arena, these benefits are priceless. Most businesses are coming to understand the value that social media brings to a brand's internal and external operations. However, some remain reluctant to jump into the fray, concerned that going social produces no easily measureable return on investment (ROI).

A recent *McKinsey Quarterly* article stated, "As the power of social media grows, it no longer makes sense to treat it as an experiment." The article argued that senior leaders can harness social media to shape consumer decision making in a predictable way:

> *Despite offering numerous opportunities to influence con-*
> *sumers, social media still accounts for less than one percent of*
> *an average marketing budget, in our experience. Many chief*
> *marketing officers say that they want to increase that share to five*
> *percent. One problem is that a lot of senior executives know little*
> *about social media. But the main obstacle is the perception that*
> *the return on investment (ROI) from such initiatives is uncertain.*
>
> *Without a clear sense of the value social media creates, it's*
> *perhaps not surprising that so many CEOs and other senior*
> *executives don't feel comfortable when their companies go*
> *beyond mere "experiments" with social-media strategy. Yet we*
> *can measure the impact of social media well beyond straight*
> *volume and consumer-sentiment metrics; in fact, we can*

*precisely determine the buzz surrounding a product or brand
and then calculate how social media drives purchasing behavior.
To do so—and then ensure that social media complements
broader marketing strategies—companies must obviously
coordinate data, tools, technology, and talent across multiple
functions. In many cases, senior business leaders must open up
their agendas and recognize the importance of supporting and
even undertaking initiatives that may traditionally have been left
to the chief marketing officer.*

*In short, today's chief executive can no longer treat social
media as a side activity run solely by managers in marketing or
public relations. It's much more than simply another form of paid
marketing, and it demands more too: a clear framework to help
CEOs and other top executives evaluate investments in it, a plan
for building support infrastructure, and performance-manage-
ment systems to help leaders smartly scale their social presence.
Companies that have these three elements in place can create
critical new brand assets (such as content from customers or
insights from their feedback), open up new channels for interactions (Twitter-based customer service, Facebook news feeds),
and completely reposition a brand through the way its employees interact with customers or other parties.* [5]

Traditional advertisers have often spoken about the "cumulative
impact" of ad campaigns. By marketing through traditional channels
such as TV, radio, billboards, bus stops, magazines, etc., the customer
could be properly primed to make a purchase decision. While this sort
of one-way pitching must be actively avoided in social media, the idea
of the cumulative impact still holds true when it comes to building
cultural capital.

The difference rests in where traditional marketing focused on
creating this impact through a persistent, monolithic message, social
engagement requires building an impact through producing and
curating rich, useful content and allowing individual employees to
champion it. Today's customer is well-informed and unafraid of voic-
ing an opinion. Customers expect the same quality of engagement

from a brand that is received from the rest of their social community. If a brand rewards them with that level of engagement, the reward will be reciprocated by the customer through increased loyalty and public advocacy.

Today, the question for businesses isn't whether a business plan should be adapted to a social blueprint, but rather how this can be achieved in a way that engages the workforce and encourages individuals to represent their brand with integrity and authenticity.

CHAPTER 3

Brands Under Pressure

As the old saying goes, "You can always tell the pioneers. They're the ones with the arrows in their backs." This might not be the most comforting of sayings to some. After all, no one really wants to be the person with a back full of arrows. However, it's worth noting in this aphorism that when all is said and done, the pioneers do emerge alive and well, arrows or not. The backs of pioneers may very well bear the marks of more difficult times, but nevertheless, they reach their destination intact and ready to fight another day.

And they do so with gumption and temerity. The arrows aren't signs of weakness; they are badges of honor. The good things both in life and in business don't—and shouldn't—come without a little bit of struggle. It's human nature to value the things we've earned more than the things we've been given. If we said the road to building an engaged base of employee brand ambassadors would be easy, not only would we be lying, we'd be doing the clients and organizations we consult a great disservice. Building a brand around social business practices is nothing short of a revolutionary act—the work of true pioneers—and that's precisely what makes the whole endeavor so worthwhile.

Make no mistake: brands are under pressure today to adapt to the changing demands of business and consumer relationships. Brands that change now can take a leadership role in the conversation. This change results in gaining influence among customers, colleagues, and—most importantly of all—social employees. As we will explore in Chapter 12, the first step is to get members of the C-Suite to buy in to these new social policies. In order for this to happen, fears must be shed, and employees must be willing to take a few arrows in the back.

The Six Most Irrational Concerns of Brands

The first step toward transitioning to a culture full of empowered social employees is to address some of the most common concerns brands face when considering going social. The following lists the most common concerns surrounding social media, as well as why these shouldn't be concerns at all.

1: Fear

There's nothing quite like good, old-fashioned fear. Everyone has heard Franklin Roosevelt's famous Depression-era quote, "The only thing we have to fear is fear itself." It's remarkable how often these words go unheeded. In truth, fear often arises out of a lack of knowledge, but brands can't afford to be ignorant in any era. Fear of social media will likely result in paranoid, overprotective, and ultimately misguided business decisions. Even worse, it will make a brand seem out of touch and unwilling to see the writing on the wall.

If brands have anything to fear, it's not social media, but losing touch with customers. Marketers need to remember that just because something is new and different doesn't mean it's bad, or even dangerous. And in all honesty, social media isn't even *that* new anymore. It's time to face the music. Brands should be aware that "I haven't done this before" only works as an excuse the first time they use it. Afterwards, they'll just start to look rigid and stubborn.

2: What If I Do It Wrong?

Many brands express misgivings as to *how* they should enter the social media fray. What if the wrong platform is chosen or organizations are not properly structured to accommodate these new technologies? On the surface, this may seem like a legitimate concern. As we've already discussed, social media certainly isn't a static entity. But no technology is. Using this same logic, brands shouldn't use computers simply because they continue to change as well.

The point is this: just because something is constantly changing doesn't mean a brand is unable to adapt right along with it. Whether it's with social media or not, brands can't avoid risk. All things considered, we believe in the old adage that there's safety in numbers. Countless brands are struggling with transitions into social business models at this very moment, and they are all learning from each other. It's better to jump in now and learn through trial and error with everyone else than to try to wait it out. If the latter is chosen, the competition will have a clear advantage over the more reticent brands.

3: Social Media Policies Don't Offer Concrete Metrics or Proven ROI

This may have been true at one point, but as you will see from our success stories in the following chapters, pioneering social businesses do indeed measure investments in social media against real returns. Even the value of contributions from individual social employees can be measured, and tremendous results are being seen. As Dion Hinchcliffe and Peter Kim say in *Social Business by Design*, "Unlike the early days of social media, results are not the problem; managing the richness and sheer scale of outcomes presents the greater business challenge."[1]

The social media versus ROI debate has actually become somewhat of a punch line in marketing circles. As much as business culture can have its own memes, the ROI conversation has certainly become one. For our favorite example, we suggest checking out "The Social Media ROI Conversation" on YouTube.

http://www.youtube.com/watch?v=qNL8vAnZ-BY

It's important to note here, however, that even though brands are finding proven ways to measure the ROI of social endeavors, it is generally agreed that ROI, in some ways, is beside the point. When talking about social business, the discussion refers to building a culture of empowered, engaged social employees who are as confident working collaboratively as they are working independently. Social business, then, is a long-term game plan for corporate sustainability, accountability, and transparency. The benefits of social business grow exponentially—and will continue to be felt for generations to come. Thinking simply in terms of ROI is, quite frankly, far too narrow a view when experiencing nothing short of a cultural revolution.

4: Inertia

When thinking of inertia in business terms, think of a brand's forward movement, or in this case, the lack thereof. It's far too easy for brands to dismiss global changes in the business world as fads, or as somehow inconsequential to their individual enterprises. Dismissive brands are content doing what they do, and have no desire to go beyond that, despite the many indicators suggesting that perhaps they should.

To a certain extent, there can be no talking sense into brands or executives who stubbornly cling to such a mindset. The truth is that the inertia mentality has been dangerous to businesses long before social media came along. Time and time again, brands have been dragged kicking and screaming into the future. Even though a fierce resistance was initially shown, most have been happy with the results. The most successful brands year in and year out are the ones ready to challenge the status quo. These are the brands that don't accept the idea that business as usual is good enough. In order to foster a culture of engaged social employees, brands must disavow the dangers of inertia directly in their mission statement—and then make sure they put their money where their mouth is.

5: Lack of Internal Structure

To many of the unindoctrinated, the idea of social business sounds like pure anarchy. Without a clear organizational hierarchy, wouldn't the whole enterprise simply descend into chaos? Let's put it this way: If a brand lacks leadership, it doesn't matter how elaborate—or sparse—its internal structure is. Without leadership, brands will lose the confidence of their employees, and if this happens there will be much larger problems to worry about.

Social business is not an argument for abandoning a structured approach to organization and collaboration. Instead, it's an argument for enriched interaction, stickier connections, and more organic collaboration. In other words, social business is about putting your employees first in order to expose and promote pockets of expertise and skill sets that tend to go unnoticed in traditional command-and-control models.

As the case studies in this book demonstrate, social businesses still maintain clearly defined roles for their employees. However, the difference is that these new social employees have much more freedom to maneuver within these roles, and they are better connected to the enterprise as a whole. To some brands, this approach might reflect the fear of losing control we addressed in Chapter 1. We think it's more important to focus on the upside of this new approach. Social brands put more trust in their employees than previous business models have allowed them to. The wonderful thing businesses are finding is that employees are almost categorically rewarding them for this newfound trust.

6: Ambiguity

This issue may actually turn out to be the root of all the other concerns we previously listed. Sure, everyone has heard the term "social media" ad nauseum at this point, but its exact meaning and application remain elusive. Social media in business extends far beyond networking platforms like Facebook and LinkedIn. As the brands in our case studies demonstrate, going social affects every aspect of business, including the way a company structures itself, communicates internally, and communicates externally. The sort of brand engagement the public sees—external social branding—is only the tip of the iceberg. If brands are afraid that the concept of social business is too big of a pill to swallow, we encourage breaking social initiatives down into more digestible pieces and tackling them one step at a time. No one can go social overnight.

Who Owns the Social Brand?

To answer the question of who owns the social brand, we have to start with the concept of ownership. This word should not be taken in the most literal sense—the question isn't a matter of trademarking or corporate charters. Rather, when we ask who owns the social brand, we are seeking to identify the people responsible for it: the individuals who drive brand value and keep its reputation in good order. Ownership, then, is representation, stewardship, and advocacy. Ownership is transforming the abstract concept of a brand into something more approachable. Who better to embody these values than the social employee?

Brand ownership wasn't always so tricky, of course. There was a time when the only thing businesses needed to be stewards of their brands was to satisfy customers with competitive products that worked the way they were supposed to and didn't gouge the customer in the process. This mindset persisted into the 1980s. By the 1990s, consumers decided this wasn't enough, and marketers responded accordingly. That decade became the era of customer *delight*, where products and services could no longer be merely satisfactory—they had to somehow transcend their physical trappings to provide the customer some greater sense of comfort.

The problem with this approach was that brands quickly joined an arms race of hyperbole, promising consumers ever-greater amounts of delight. Inevitably these claims of boundless delight ran their course, and these brand promises naturally began to ring hollow. Companies may still have owned their brand identities, but consumers had become indifferent to the whole process.

Brand ownership in the twenty-first century still maintains lofty goals as it did in the 1990s. However, the new buzzwords—inspiration, loyalty, and advocacy—actually appear attainable. Brand ownership has moved far beyond products and into the realm of idealism, albeit idealism firmly rooted in practical business techniques. Whether it's Zappos's slogan "Delivering Happiness" or IBM's "Smarter Planet," brands have sights set on the broad horizon of the future— and they just might make it there. Simon Sinek probably said it best in a 2009 TED talk, "People don't buy what you do. They buy why you do it."[2] As brands move further into the second decade of this young century, many are retooling the idea of brand ownership around this very concept in order to inspire both customer and employee loyalty.

http://www.ted.com/talks/simon_sinek_how_great_leaders_inspire_action.html

Employee Voice as Brand Identity

Today's consumers expect online engagement with brands, and they expect to be engaged in an authentic manner. Consumers don't want to speak to a brand; they want to speak to real people. The rules of engagement for interpersonal interaction between social employees and customers are still largely unwritten. It is a certainty that employee voices matter, and that a brand's reputation depends tremendously on how well its social employee representatives communicate with the outside world.

The truly engaged social employee does not *play* at engagement in order to appease the public and make them go away. Again, if brands are serious about establishing a culture of authentic communication, such a mindset would be toxic to that environment. The social employee must understand that open, earnest communication goes beyond simple salesmanship. However, before these employees can represent their brands externally, they must first learn how to communicate well internally.

This is the true secret to the success of the social business model, and the result—brands with purpose—is well worth it. This approach requires an unprecedented amount of trust in a brand's social employees, but that is precisely why the conversation must begin in-house so that the employees can learn the power of their own voices and how to share that power with the outside world.

Your Employees Already Own Your Brand

Brand engagement does not begin in the public sphere, nor does it begin at the front doors of the corporate office. It begins at the desks of social employees and spreads outward through the network like wildfire. Social business affects every aspect of a brand's everyday operations. David Armano, managing director at Edelman Digital Chicago, stated:

> *In order for a business to truly extract value from social initiatives, we must consider not only marketing but how it impacts research and development, human resources, innovation, business intelligence and other facets of an organization which help drive a business forward.*[3]

A brand's employees stand at the frontline of customer communication and internal collaboration. They are responsible for representing a brand's message and values, day in and day out. In the social age, this fact is simply unavoidable. It's the brand's job, therefore, to ensure that its employees carry this message out into the world responsibly and accurately.

In order to achieve this goal, brands must ensure that their management teams understand and support employee empowerment initiatives. Even in social business, brand vision should originate from the C-Suite. Input from employees and management can—and should—be solicited. Employees are more likely to buy into an initiative and become stakeholders if afforded an opportunity to contribute.

In this way, executives will act as sieves, sorting out the tangible ideas from the less concrete suggestions. With these shared ideals established, a brand's mission must be accurately and uniformly communicated across all departments. Representatives from each of the brands appearing in this book had different ways of approaching this challenge, but they all recognized the idea that strong Business-to-Business (B2B) or Business-to-Consumer (B2C) communication outside of the brand's walls begins with strong internal employee collaboration. By embracing this necessary first step, companies can ensure brand identities are placed in good hands.

Marketing Is Everyone's Job

Because of the many new demands that social media has created for internal organization as well as B2B and B2C interactions, brands are quickly coming to the realization that the act of marketing is no longer just the responsibility of the marketing department. Knowledge of products and services will continue to be specialized, and with consumers expecting easy access to information, the inescapable truth is that the people best suited to talk about a product or service are the people who produced it. This isn't to say that each member of each department has to be on the frontlines of branding, just that everybody should have a role in spreading the brand's message. This could be as simple as maintaining strong internal collaboration across departments to make sure everyone's calendars are lining up, or it could mean running either an internal or an external blog speaking to some aspect of the brand.

This revolutionary idea for marketing makes for both better products and richer engagement. Marketing becomes less about promoting an item and more about putting fresh ideas to work. Many of the representative companies we spoke with reported that some of the most innovative ideas over the past few years have come from what would traditionally have been unlikely sources, thanks to improved collaboration opportunities between departments that had previously been walled off from one another. Allowing social employees greater input into the production and marketing process will not only yield surprising results, it will yield a greater stake in the results for those employees.

Power of Social Media

Social media has also created another very intriguing reality for brands and employees, as organizations are no longer limited to a physical structure, or even proximity. The only thing preventing organizations from connecting employees with the necessary information and resources to drive real change is the willingness to develop a proper infrastructure. The percentage of remote employees in the workforce is growing each year.[4] With this change comes a whole list of other organizational questions that brands must be able to answer. Many companies simply don't know how to handle the changes in the work styles and attitudes that are emerging within the workforce.

The power of social media is that the path can be cocreated by brands, the brand's employees, and the customers connected to the brand. Social business allows for a two-way street, leading to richer, more nuanced discussions. In other words, brands don't need to have all the answers before setting out on the social journey. Empower the collaborators of a brand, and the brand will be enriched.

CHAPTER 4

The Social Employee– Lines Blur Between Brands, Employees, and Customers

In a world where brand identity is now cocreated by brands, employees, and customers, the traditional lines used to distinguish these groups continue to blur. Social employees work to embody a brand's ideals and message without compromising their own personal brands. Each of us contributes to the branding process whether as employees or as consumers. This tends to make us as willing to advocate on behalf of others as we are to advocate on behalf of ourselves.

This cultural exchange continues to grow in complexity, and as a result many brands are unsure of what roles should be encompassed in this new social landscape. Some brands have chosen to dive right into the fray with the hope that the path will become a little clearer once they're in the thick of things. For the most part, they've been right to do so. Social branding can't be forced. This is the reason individual contribution marks the essential difference between talking the talk and walking the walk.

The Social Employee Drives Social Business

The ultimate goal of any brand is to earn the trust and repeat business of a large consumer base. In turn, this builds brand value and ultimately leads to profit. Social branding isn't just a component of this process; it *is* the process. In the previous chapters, we've made the case that a brand's external reality reflects its internal one. A brand can't present a unified front to the public if it can't produce the same for its employees. More succinctly, if each employee who plays a part in shaping a brand's identity has a different idea of what passes for acceptable social etiquette and brand advocacy, the brand risks appearing schizophrenic in the public eye.

In this chapter we will dive into the world of social employees, exploring defining characteristics, primary drivers, and why social employees can be a brand's greatest asset if properly utilized. Brands that have a clearly defined mission, and drive that message from the top down, will reap the benefits of a unified social culture where the individual voices of each employee ring out as one. For this to be achieved, a company must put brand and employee culture above all other organizational considerations. Define the culture, and drive the conversation.

Social business models are the templates of the future. Not every brand will approach the concept of social media in the same way, and each will choose different internal structures that best match set goals. Regardless of how a brand chooses to get there, it is clear that the movement has already begun.

Social Employees Orbit the Brand

When considering terms like "social business" and "social employee," it's important to consider how these concepts work in relation to each other. While social business is the end goal, the social employee is the brand's faithful guide. The two depend a great deal on each other, but they can also exist outside of each other. Social employees can be found at social businesses as well as traditional command-and-control businesses.

While it's true that the social employee will feel more empowered while working for the former rather than the latter, in either case, work will be approached with a particular skill set and outlook that

Figure 4.1

—— THINK OF A BRAND AS A PLANET ——

Drawing social employees into orbit through its core values

Credit: Blue Focus Marketing®

will define the ways in which collaboration with fellow employees and customers takes place. Whatever the case may be, the social employee and the social business form an intricate system with each other. This system is based on mutual exchange rather than mutual dependence.

Think of social employees as satellites, and brands as planets. Each satellite exists as its own entity, but the gravity generated by the brand pulls these separate units into a larger interactive system. The better a brand defines its identity, values, and culture, the stronger its gravity will be—and the greater pull it will have on each employee. Employees who identify with a brand's core values will be thrilled at the prospect of contributing to innovative new projects. As a result, these types of employees are far less likely to "break orbit" from their brands (see Figure 4.1).

A Culture of Empowerment

What does this mean for businesses? At the very least, it means that in the twenty-first century, brands have a responsibility to employees to establish acceptable guidelines for social conduct. As more members of the millennial generation enter the workforce, this necessity will only increase. To extend the brand-as-planet metaphor, companies that do not engage employees through collaborative platforms will fail to generate the kind of gravity necessary to keep employees in orbit. As a result, these companies will lose out to other more dynamic brands that produce a stronger pull.

Make no mistake, the path to the social business lies through empowering the social employee. It can't be any other way. Social business is all about building a culture of seamless collaboration across channels. The catch is this: you can't fake culture. Without a strong buy-in across all levels of the business, brands will just be going through the motions. The tools and the protocols will be in place, but the driving force that puts all these tools in motion—employee engagement—will be absent. Many brands echo the same sentiment: all the toys in the world won't increase productivity if the employees don't know how to integrate these tools into their workflow.

As things stand now, the number of brands that have successfully implemented social employee policies can fit on the tip of an arrow. However, these few brave pioneers report inspiring results: increased flexibility that doesn't sacrifice accountability, dynamic conversations that don't drown out individual voices, and democratic structures that prize the best ideas.

Customers as Brand Ambassadors

True brand advocacy doesn't end with the employees—it begins with them. The social employee may be a satellite connected to a larger system, but each satellite also maintains independent interconnected networks. The social employee's job becomes one of making the brand's message more granular—a message full of personality and character, capable of resonating in unique and unpredictable ways.

Accessibility is the name of the game in exchanges such as these. Successful social employees can embody a brand's message with both coworkers and customers by demonstrating a personal investment in the brand and its services. Through this form of organic, authentic engagement, social employees can make their message accessible to numerous groups of people, who will in turn spread the message to their own social channels.

A recent eMarketer survey found that 50 percent of all customers are actually quite eager to forward a brand's message if their own customer experience was enjoyable. Further, while literally half of all customers are willing to advocate based on a good experience, another 37 percent will advocate products to help friends and family, while only 1 percent advocate for personal gain such as rewards and discounts.[1]

This sort of advocacy is not only inexpensive, but incredibly powerful. As eMarketer writer/analyst Kimberly Maul stated, "Because the average consumer inherently trusts his or her friends and family, a person who is a brand advocate can be highly influential. And advocates are stepping up to that opportunity."[2] The catch is that trust has to be earned, and the only way to achieve this consistently is by developing social business structures that put employees on the front lines.

The Rise of the Personal Brand

Here we see an excellent example of the blurred distinction between customer and employee. Through public or semipublic platforms such as blogs, Twitter, or LinkedIn, individuals often wear many different hats throughout the course of the day. One moment a person might be singing the praises of a particular product they just purchased, and in the next moment sharing information relevant to their industry. The identities a person inhabits in the social sphere can be incredibly mutable.

This can cause no small amount of hand wringing among the higher-ups of certain brands. What if these employees share sensitive information about the brand? What if they paint the brand in a bad light? What if their personal views don't reflect the views of the company? These are all very good questions, which is why we strongly recommend that businesses do a little soul searching before embarking on their social journeys.

As it turns out, the personal brand—an individual's digital social identity—is a tremendous asset for businesses. Whereas the business world has often operated under the assumption that individual character traits are to be suppressed in favor of a more homogenized brand identity, social media has turned this assumption on its head. Character matters. This push for individuality is coming from both the consumer and employee ends of the spectrum. On the one side, many employees are leery of appearing as if they're simply some anonymous cog in a machine, blandly toeing the company line. On the other hand, because of the rich nature of exchange customers enjoy as a part of social media with other friends and acquaintances, they expect their interactions with brands to reflect this same level of depth. Customers don't want to talk to a one-dimensional sales machine; they want to talk to a real person who thinks real thoughts in real time.

One popular term for this kind of person is the "brandividual." In essence, brandividuals give brands a human face in online interactions. They leverage public perceptions of both their own personal brands and their employers' brands as a means of generating authenticity, trust, and goodwill. As David Armano wrote in his now-famous blog post:

> For each brand on Twitter, there's an individual (or individuals) behind that effort. It's both business and personal. The two have become one. The tactic comes from a fundamental truth when it comes to the social spaces on the Web. People want to talk to other people. They want transparency. They want to know who they are talking to.[3]

Personal branding precisely allows for this kind of interaction. Employees largely get to be themselves. As long as everyone agrees on the proper framework for these interactions, individually empowered brandividuals can improve the image of a brand through their own rich interactions, helpfulness, and engaging personalities. They bring credibility and esteem to their parent brands by putting their own skills on display through blogs, content sharing, retweets, and professional public profiles on platforms like LinkedIn. By demonstrating their own personal worth through personal branding, these employees become external reflections of their thriving corporate cultures.

How Do You Know a Social Employee When You See One?

Companies seeking to identify their existing roster of social employees often don't know where to start. How does one distinguish a social employee from a "traditional" employee? Do these employees look or dress differently? Do they have some kind of secret handshake they use to keep the uninitiated at arm's length?

In reality, the social employee tends to hide in plain sight. It may be easy to spot social employees in the digital realm, but sometimes it is more difficult to identify them in the workplace. The truth is, because the business world is still waking up to social collaboration techniques, social employees aren't always aware they're doing anything different or groundbreaking. Instead, these employees see social tools as pragmatic solutions to the challenges that confront them throughout the course of a normal day. They don't see social media as an additional burden to pile onto the workday, but rather as a solution for streamlining what would otherwise be time-consuming processes.

Social employees are comfortable with digital collaborative environments, having used these tools at home for years. They are early adopters of technology, and accustomed to working in unstable, ever-changing environments. For the more advanced social employees, applying these tools to solve their problems is as simple as breathing: it serves an essential need, but there's nothing particularly challenging about it.

These kinds of employees are usually wonderful assets for business teams, as they tend to take it upon themselves to provide the group with the right collaborative tools for a particular need. They are unafraid of developing their own processes in order to get a job done, and don't feel the need to constantly ask for direction. These sorts of social employee initiatives often mark the first steps a brand takes toward becoming a social business, although the steps themselves are often unknown to the brands until much later.

Seven Characteristics of the Social Employee

1: Engaged

We lead off with this trait because it forms the keystone in the arch of social employee traits. Without engagement, the whole arch falls apart. The ultimate goal of the social business is to be able to provide excellent customer service through rich, authentic communications. As stated earlier, if authenticity can't be faked, a culture of employees who are simply motivated rather than engaged won't cut it. Motivation puts the food on the table, but engagement fosters a certain pride and sense of usefulness that is not only personally gratifying, but beneficial to brands in the social era.

2: Expects Integration of the Personal and Professional

The lines between brands, employees, and customers have all been effectively blurred. This kind of ambiguity can cause anxiety for some, but the social employee doesn't see any conflict. More digital natives are entering the workforce every day. These young workers and the generation from which they've emerged expect the negotiation between their personal lives and their professional lives to be a simple one.

This isn't to say that they *demand* it—that's far too strong a word. Rather, they expect it, because they simply don't know how to be any other way. These digital natives, labeled by many as the millennial generation, have grown up in a time where individuality and personal expression aren't simply tolerated, but encouraged. They aren't used to stifling their bold personalities for just anyone, and often become somewhat flustered when encountering environments that don't facilitate this kind of expression.

We should note as well that millennials don't hold all the keys to the social employee castle. As we will illustrate in Chapter 12, social employees must exist at all levels of an organization, from senior leadership and down through the ranks. The truth is that members of any generational group can be—and are—social employees. We specifically mention the millennials to illustrate the increasing need for social philosophies to be adopted in businesses as this new generation continues to enter the workforce in ever growing numbers.

The social employee exists in a time when even the traditional eight-hour workday isn't a guaranteed fixture. As the amounts of portable technologies and remote workers increase, social employees have the tools to work in environments far removed from the traditional office space. Today's employees don't accept the idea that lifestyles must be completely retooled around a job. This isn't to say that an unstructured, set-your-own-rules kind of environment is expected, just that work hours and location are much more negotiable than they used to be.

The social business isn't threatened by the big personalities of its social employees or the changing nature of the physical work environment. While more freedom may be inherent in the social business model, this is not an argument for anarchy, and new challenges certainly arise from the integration of the personal with the professional. For this reason, brands must be proactive in establishing their cultural DNA and providing operational guidelines early in the social adoption process. Social employees expect latitude, not free rein of the company.

3: Buys into the Brand's Story

As we discussed in Chapter 1, storytelling is one of the hottest buzzwords in the marketing community right now. Often the value of storytelling is expressed in relation to the consumer. Because of this, its value to the employee goes overlooked. The challenge is this: if customer buy-in depends on authentic storytelling, and if brand advocacy is moving further and further into the realm of the social employee, then employee buy-in is just as essential as consumer buy-in. To advocate effectively, social employees have to believe in what they're selling.

Once again, this process starts from the inside before working its way out. Employee advocates must know the brand's story inside and out before engaging customers. One of our favorite examples of inspirational storytelling and its relationship to effective marketing is Coca-Cola. This brand has brilliantly articulated its position on the subject with a few visionary videos that are freely available on YouTube. If you have about 20 minutes, we suggest watching them for yourself.

Coca-Cola Content 2020 Part One

http://www.youtube.com/watch?v=LerdMmWjU_E

Coca-Cola Content 2020 Part Two

http://www.youtube.com/watch?v=_hXPnb3PjsE

4: Born Collaborator

While we can all admit that there's a certain pride that comes from being able to say "I thought of that," sometimes taking this "me first" mentality can dramatically slow down the creative process. Social employees understand that an idea's origin is far less important than the idea itself. Traditionally, employees have tended to hoard their ideas, afraid that someone else might take credit for their brilliance. After all, whoever gets credit for the idea gets the promotion. In this way, creativity is as good as currency. This mentality may appear to benefit individual self-interest, but in reality it slows down the entire process of critical thinking. In turn, brand innovation is reduced to a glacial pace.

Champions of the "me first" mentality forget one crucial element: the greatest by-product of a good idea is more good ideas.

Social businesses can be a wellspring of new ideas, but the "me first" mentality directly inhibits this kind of culture. Social employees understand the power of crowd thinking, and that this type of process can drive innovation at an incredibly accelerated pace. In a culture where good ideas are both celebrated and quickly disseminated, new ideas are always sure to follow. In this way, everyone benefits, because everyone contributes.

The most cutting-edge brands already understand this. For instance, companies like Facebook and Google regularly host "hack-athons" in which developers are essentially placed in a room together and tasked with developing new ideas for company platforms. In February 2011, Foursquare hosted a 15-hour event that resulted in the development of 39 new apps for their platform.[4] This kind of productivity is only possible through a culture of noncompetitive collaboration, where the best idea wins out regardless of its source.

5: Listens

Listening is a dynamic activity. We pay it a lot of lip service in the marketing world, but it's often the first thing to slip our minds. For many, the first impulse when representing a brand is to embellish themselves and the products, forcibly inserting a personal agenda into the center of the conversation. The social employee understands that even the simple act of being courteous can encourage consumer interest in a brand. By taking the time to understand where bosses, coworkers, and customers are coming from, social employees can offer feedback that isn't a canned response, but tailored to a specific situation.

Social media channels offer us many new ways to listen—from emails to wikis, tweets to status updates. Listening should not be considered a passive activity. Listening is not waiting for your turn to talk, nor is it tuning out until the other person is finished speaking. The social employee *actively* listens by asking questions, seeking feedback, and looking for conversations where their contributions might be valued. Regardless of the type of communication, a company that actively listens will be much better positioned to establish rich business relationships with employees and customers alike. As the question of big data looms large in the business world, active listening must be present at every level.

6: Customer-Centric

This one should be a no-brainer. We're certainly not saying anything new when we stress the value of the customer. However, being customer-centric must go further than simple platitudes like "the customer is always right." At the very least, this statement is adversarial. It implies a standoff of sorts. For someone to be right, someone else has to be wrong. Such an outcome is fine if the two parties are engaged in a debate, but business communication in the twenty-first century prizes a helpful, informed exchange above all else. It's not about being right or wrong, but rather emerging better informed as a result of the exchange.

The social employee understands that every customer is an employee somewhere, and that every coworker is a customer in many other places as well. No one likes feeling ignored or otherwise disregarded by a brand. The rise of social media means that every employee with a Twitter profile is a de facto brand ambassador. Social employees are not only aware of this, they work to maximize its impact. By prizing authentic engagement and rich exchanges, the social employee is able to leverage virtual platforms toward real-world results.

7: Empowered Change Agent

Businesses can't reasonably update organizational structures if employees aren't driving change at every level. Because of this, the term "change agent" should be a part of every employee's job description. This term only paints half of the picture, however. The social employee must be comfortable acting as a change agent long after the employer has adopted a social business model. Going social is an ongoing process. The best practices and best platforms for internal collaboration will continue to evolve, and brands must continue to do so with them.

Driving change is everyone's job, and it affects all levels of business. Brands don't need to follow each new trend down a rabbit hole, but employees should be enabled to act as change agents when better ways of doing things are derived. The social business empowers the social employee by creating the proper space for change.

Going Social from the Bottom Up

Many brands often begin to go social in a bottom-up manner, where the employees themselves take the lead in adopting change. While this sort of agency should be prized at brands both large and small, this process does present some challenges. The most pressing challenge to face is silos sprouting up around these employees and their departments. If employees begin to improvise, the situation becomes somewhat of a catch-22. Consider a situation where the employee utilizes social collaboration tools to improve group communication and workflow. In so doing, the entire group or department is then benefited. This contributes to the short-term success of the brand.

However, as the old saying goes, there's more than one way to cook an egg. If small pockets of workers throughout the company create social solutions independently of other workers, they'll all end up with different kinds of eggs—or different solutions to the same problems. Once this has happened, groups and departments may be better at communicating with their immediate coworkers, but their ability to collaborate companywide will inevitably face new hurdles. This challenge strikes at the heart of why businesses must develop a comprehensive social media policy. If they don't, the question won't go away. Instead, their employees will simply improvise.

As we said in the last chapter, marketing is everyone's job. If this is true, and if it's also true that successful marketing efforts depend on incisive communication and coordination skills, then it stands to reason that effective communication is also everyone's job. Social employees understand this, which is why steps have been taken within each department to put effective communication policies in place. However, from where they are within a company, these employees do not have the influence, power, or resources to effect a global change in culture or structure. So, while employees help to build awareness of new social tools from the bottom up, brands must be ready to set the tone and rules of engagement from the top down.

The next section of our book explores the ways in which leading brands have championed this process, reconfiguring their businesses for a future where change reigns as the new normal.

PART II

How Great Companies Build Social Cultures

CHAPTER 5

IBM–Making Connections One Employee at a Time

One common trait found among the companies we interviewed was their progressive stance on adopting new technologies and business models a little ahead of the curve. In the mid-1990s, many Internet networking practices began to take root in our culture. Several companies responded with fear, implementing a variety of rules, programs, and procedures designed to prevent employees from using the web while at work. IBM took a different route, choosing instead to adopt a permissive stance.

IBM trusted employees to use the web not just responsibly, but as a tool for day-to-day tasks. To some outsiders, it may have appeared that IBM was taking a big risk by granting employees so much latitude. However, the venture ended up becoming the brand's most important step into the transparent, connected social business world of the twenty-first century.

The culture that IBM fostered is a proud one. "IBMers," as they like to call themselves, work in an integrated social environment where they are confident their contributions will be heard. These social employees deeply trust their networks of colleagues, managers, and clients and work tirelessly to find social solutions for common business challenges. IBM isn't just a social business. IBM just might become the model for social business success over the next decade.[1]

Employees Are the Brand

To Ethan McCarty, Director of Enterprise Social Strategy at IBM, a social brand defines itself by its skills and flexibility in connecting with potential clients, thought leaders, or brand advocates. Employees at brands like IBM build communities by generating captivating content that is both helpful and engaging. Social employees catalyze the brand and respond to individual needs by making empowered decisions.

In describing the relationship between the social business and the social employee, McCarty provided the following analogy:

> Picture a ball and a bag of marbles side by side. The two items might have the same volume—that is, if you dropped them in a bucket, they would displace the same amount of water. The difference, however, lies in the surface area. Because a bag of marbles is comprised of several individual pieces, the combined surface area of all the marbles far outstrips the surface area of a single ball. This expanded surface area represents a social brand's increased diversity. These surfaces connect and interact with each other in unique ways, offering customers and employees alike a variety of paths towards a myriad of solutions. If none of the paths prove to be suitable, social employees can carve out new paths on their own.

As McCarty stated, employees *are* the brand at IBM. Their value lies in the multitude of possible connections and ideas that over 400,000 marbles can collectively produce.

Managing the Brand by Establishing Values

According to Ben Edwards, Vice President of Global Communications and Digital Marketing at IBM, the practice of brand management as a whole has only recently been pushed to align the image a company presents externally with the culture it fosters internally.

Traditionally, brand management tended to be concerned with questions of advertising, logos, stationery, and the decorations in the lobby of a corporate office. These types of elements are starting to seem superficial in today's content-rich media environment. Decorations and stationery may be aesthetically pleasing, but in order to build thriving B2B relationships, today's brands must leverage mission, vision, and values in the marketplace.

Edwards also noted that the move toward transparency has demanded a deeper, more comprehensive definition of brand management on all touch points—upstream into the supply chain, downstream into the client base, and everywhere in between.

> *Our contention is that the core of brand management is about aligning the values of the employee, client, business partner, and everybody that interacts with the company with the corporate character itself. And if you do that well, you activate the brand in amazingly powerful ways.*

Edwards also stated that the truly social business doesn't just align its values with the values of its employees—a truly social business integrates those values. One essential by-product of social media's ubiquitous arrival on the scene is the rise of the employee brand. Social employees are eager to represent brands on social channels such as Twitter or LinkedIn, but they must first understand how their values intersect with the values of the organization.

The best employees seek out companies with a firmly established set of brand values. A brand's commitment to these values is ultimately reflected in the culture it produces. To ensure corporate values are aligned with the values of its employees, executives at IBM have kept the conversation ongoing, encouraging employees to contribute to and express those values within the work environment.

Initial Challenges

In order to activate and drive social employee engagement, the executives at IBM wanted to instill the idea that all aspects of the brand were built to last. As a major provider of B2B services, IBM wanted to be sure its products were built around the idea of enduring relationships. IBM knew the production of industry-leading products couldn't be only about tech—it would have to extend to people and processes as well. According to Edwards, when a client chooses to engage with an IBMer, they know that the employee is in it for long-term success.

When IBM began upgrading its social networking capabilities in 2005, executives understood the new tools wouldn't be driving the change—but rather their effect on brand culture. To ensure a successful shift toward a more social culture, employees would need to rally around a shared vision of what social meant to each of them (see Figure 5.1).

Taking the Question to the People

In trying to determine the best way to address questions regarding the proper protocols of a social business, IBM struck on a novel idea: rather than confining a small group of people to a conference room to hammer out social policy, why not take the questions to the people? IBM quickly decided to set up an open wiki accessible to the entire

Figure 5.1   How to Use Social Business for Social Branding

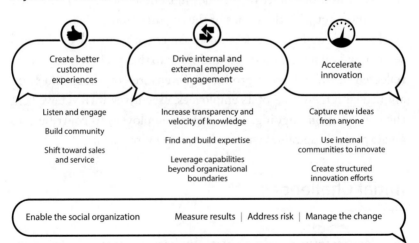

Credit: IBM

network that would allow IBMers to establish their own computing guidelines.

An approach like this demonstrates the fundamental power of internal crowdsourcing as a means of problem solving. Instead of relying on small groups of people to work tirelessly through the nuances of comprehensive policy development, IBM was able to rely on the vast intellectual resources of its employee base. By trading in the ball for the bag of marbles, the company was able to achieve an incredibly rich document. Furthermore, this recursive approach put into practice the very principles IBM was hoping to instill—making the experience itself an example of the desired outcome.

As Ethan McCarty stated:

It was a really magical moment. We were filled with people who were good citizens, and who believed in progress—that's why they came to IBM in the first place. Through this document, IBM put a flag in the ground early on for very broad participation.

The document rewarded the employees' standards of social propriety and set the stage for social media exploration. In all, over 200 employees contributed to the document, most of whom were not affiliated with IBM's Communications Department. The guidelines extended far beyond the dos and don'ts of social engagement and included concepts of transparency, etiquette, and the values of authentic communication.

The results of the wiki experiment were quickly adapted as the company's official social media guidelines. According to McCarty, everything is still holding up quite well. "IBMers treat it like their Magna Carta. They're really into what it says about their company," he says. The guidelines, which McCarty affectionately refers to as IBM's social media Woodstock, have become so renowned in the business world that hundreds of other organizations have contacted IBM seeking permission to adopt them as their own. Speaking as an exemplar of a social executive thriving in a shifting landscape, McCarty said, "It has been our great pleasure to serve as a model for these organizations."

To learn more about this document, which was too big to print here, we strongly recommend visiting the source itself at: http://www.ibm.com/blogs/zz/en/guidelines.html.

Credit: http://www.ibm.com/blogs/zz/en/guidelines.html

The Digital IBMer Hub

After IBM established guidelines for social engagement, the next task was to put policy into practice. Coordinating over 400,000 employees spread out over 170 countries was certainly no small feat. IBM may have been a bag of marbles in the world of social business, but the brand had to make sure it didn't "lose all its marbles" during the adoption process. Employees would have to be trained in the brand's new guidelines to ensure integration into brand culture.

The Digital IBMer Hub is essentially the first tier in the process of employee enablement (see Figure 5.2). A resource such as this educates IBMers on the various social initiatives within the brand. The program seeks to enable employees to participate in and live the IBM values in the digital world. Employees in the program learn how to use social computing tools to collaborate, read and distribute news, and build engaged networks. The Hub's offerings extend beyond courses, providing employees with easy access to essential guidelines, policies, and training models as well.

The process is entirely opt-in, though it is incentivized through internal course credit, recognition, and other rewards. Because IBM employees tend to be socially engaged and eager to learn new approaches to communication and problem solving, McCarty reported that participation in the program is largely self-driven. This

Figure 5.2

Credit: IBM

trait distinguishes IBM from numerous other brands. Furthermore, the self-paced learning design of the program reduces any intimidation factor, and the company's recommendation engine software helps guide employees where to go once a particular course has been finished.

Motivation Through Rewards and Recognition

Gamification

In the younger employee ranks of genXers and millennials, the ideas of "leveling up" and "completing missions" essential to video game culture have become so ingrained in the way challenges are approached that architects of the Digital IBMer program worked to integrate such concepts into training models. Sandy Carter, Vice President of Social Business Sales at IBM and recipient of our 2012 #Nifty50 Award for

Women in Technology on Twitter, began a gamification program as an external outreach effort to teach customers about new tech tools.

Carter and others within the company quickly began to see the value of earning badges in regard to company training. The strength of gamification is its ability to promote desired behaviors and outcomes by incentivizing them in the process.

Who Wouldn't Want a Balloon?

Aside from gamification, IBM has other programs in place to ensure employees are recognized and rewarded for their efforts. In IBM's Digital Eminence Awards, for instance, sales representatives who model the right behaviors are rewarded by their managers with items such as a certificate of recognition, a box of chocolates, or even a day off. When we spoke with Jennifer Dubow, Social Business Inside Sales Transformation Leader at IBM, she noted that the real value in these programs is not the reward itself, but the public recognition and visibility of being acknowledged as being valuable to a program.

Dubow used the analogy of a balloon to illustrate why recognition is so powerful. Balloons are cheap and serve no real purpose, but if an associate has a balloon sticking out of their workspace, they know that they're the only one in the room with a balloon. No one else has a balloon, but everybody else can see the associate's balloon from across the floor. In essence, it's the recognition that counts, that opportunity to be proud of their accomplishments and the value they generate for the brand (see Figure 5.3).

Of course, Dubow is also quick to point out that often the successes in applying one's knowledge to real business outcomes can be a reward in itself. To illustrate this, Dubow mentioned a particular instance where an IBMer had a difficult time trying to reach a client. After numerous attempts trying to contact the client via phone and email, the employee reached out on LinkedIn and received a response almost immediately. This experience may seem small, but for employees learning new best practices for meaningful engagement, a positive outcome like this will reinforce training and illustrate the value of social processes.

Figure 5.3

Credit: Blue Focus Marketing

Connections—IBM's Portal to the Social Stratosphere

Once IBM established what social business models meant to employee culture, it was up to the technology giant to design a platform capable of bringing social computing to the employee's everyday work experience. Through a social initiative known as the Technology Adoption Program (TAP; see later in the chapter), initial ideas for an enterprise-wide social media platform known as Connections came about.

Through TAP, social IBMers throughout the company contributed ideas to Connections' development—regardless of whether those employees worked in the technology department or not. IBMers began honing their own collaboration skills and contributing to social culture while simultaneously expanding the company's internal networking capabilities.

Connections was designed to integrate worker and group activity streams, calendaring, wikis, blogs, email functions, and data analytics. Employees are able to access Connections while at work, at home, or on the go with cloud-based, company-wide integration. Perhaps most importantly, employees can collaborate either one-on-one or through the creation of secure communities—some of which extend outside the organization. For a major B2B provider like IBM, this kind of internal/external flexibility has proven to be very useful.

Connections also collects and organizes tremendous amounts of data generated from people, devices, and other external sensors, providing IBMers with rich analysis and insights capabilities. IBM uses these data-capture features to help discover and predict essential patterns that might lead to market shifts. Employees can also track the path and transmission of essential data through integrated, customizable newsfeeds. Finally, Connections integrates features for photo sharing, geo location, tagging, and ideation capabilities that allow employees to either comment or vote on ideas in a community—creating seamless internal crowdsourcing capabilities.

Making Connections with B2B Businesses

Connections Product Manager Suzanne Livingston has overseen the program's development from the beginning stages of using it as an internal tool to becoming one of the brand's products. Many other businesses worldwide now use IBM's Connections software for their own social networking needs. IBM works directly with brands to make sure their Connections platform is fully integrated and scalable within different business environments.

International Data Corporation (IDC) has ranked IBM number one in the world market share for enterprise social software for three consecutive years, with no signs of slowing down.[2] In fact, over 60 percent of Fortune 100 companies have licensed Connections and other solutions for social business. One major selling point for the Connections software is its capacity for industry-leading analytics software. IBM is meeting the challenge presented by big data by investing over $14 billion in analytics acquisitions over the past five years. Recent enterprise software clients include Lowe's Home Improvement, Electrolux, TD Bank Group, and Bayer Material Science (see Figure 5.4).

Integrated Workflow

According to John Rooney, Technical Strategy Leader at IBM, the benefit of crowdsourcing Connections through employees was their becoming invested in the success of the platform by being allowed to contribute organically to its development. Because of this, the creation of Connections wasn't product-led, but driven by what different individuals and teams from across the company needed to be successful, innovative, and engaged in all activities. Rooney said, "Aligning the way you deploy those tools to your culture is what's going to help you succeed. That is why we make this the foundation of what we offer to clients."

Connections has a diverse and ever-expanding set of tools designed to give IBMers everything needed to become socially integrated within the company. Through IBM intranet's home page, known as W3, employees are offered news stories and other information based on an employee's specific job role and geography. As Rooney said, "When you come to your homepage in the morning, you get a full glance of your day—from corporate activities to your immediate community networks."

Each employee has an individual profile. This profile includes colleague contact information, internal status updates, filesharing, wikis and other shared documents, activities, and communities of interest. Connections is also integrated along an instant messaging network. The Connections media library allows employees to share audio and video—providing instant access to recordings of meetings and multimedia blogging materials. Rooney noted that IBM management even turned to video blogging as a means of communicating with employees.

Figure 5.4   The State of Social Technology Adoption in Businesses Today

What is the state of social technologies in your organization?

IBM surveyed 1,160 business and IT professionals to understand the state of social business adoption to take a pulse on how organizations are tapping the power of social technologies to advance business objectives.

The value of social business is increasing within organizations.

46%

of the companies surveyed increased their social business investments in 2012.

Companies that are emerging as social business leaders are applying the technologies to drive customer-facing activities such as lead generation, sales and post-sales service.

Despite the accelerated adoption of social technologies, **middle managers** who are being called on to implement these technologies are facing challenges.

2/3

of respondents are not sure they **sufficiently understand the impact** that social technologies would have on their organizations over the next three years.

There are different perspectives within management. Only 22 percent believe that middle managers are prepared to incorporate social technologies into their daily practices, while 48 percent of organizations indicate they have support from the C-Suite.

22%
Middle Managers

48%
C-Suite

For organizations to evolve into social enterprises, some basic groundwork must be laid.

Provide an infrastructure for engagement like setting up forums, teamrooms and collaborative spaces.

Integrated social practices into day-to-day work activities like using blog posts and activity streams to positively accentuate project management tasks.

Understand where and how data generation could benefit the enterprise.

Teach employees how to collaborate effectively with individuals outside of the organization's boundaries using social business methods and tools.

Credit: IBM (IBM IBV Social Business Adoption Study 2012)

Employees at the brand continually improve the Connections experience. Much of the recent work has been focused on building applications into business practices. One such focus is customer relationship management (CRM). By integrating this process into the Connections system, employees have easier access to rich data on IBM clients. The inclusion of clients into these systems through external/internal hybrid communities only further enhances the process. The goal is to make foundational services more enabled through the social network in order to bring social behaviors directly to the specific work tasks.

Authentic Connections

Ethan McCarty described IBMers as working in a very federated way. Although expected to follow IBM's guidelines, employees' social activities are not centrally managed. This allows authentic dialogue to come about organically. According to IBM, over 400,000 employees engage the public, clients, and customers either through IBM-owned platforms like Connections or external platforms such as LinkedIn, Twitter, and Facebook. Subject experts now regularly encounter customers and the public through blogs and digital hangouts.

IBMers understand they have a duty to respond to social media inquiries from a variety of channels in a timely manner. However, with hundreds of thousands of employees at the company, there can be no ambiguity as to who should respond to specific messages. When we asked Suzanne Livingston how response protocols are handled, she replied that this duty was largely federated as well:

> As is the case with most of our social tools, the community is often the moderator. They are the ones to oversee how things work. So, the question of who answers messages on Twitter is kind of self-governing. For instance, if there is a question regarding Connections on Twitter, it is expected that either myself or my team is going to answer it. It's a flexible model because that

is the way that social works—it is not fixed. It is not a top-down governance or hierarchy of what has to happen—we organize as best we can for the situation.

Rather than thinking about social media as a mechanism for content, IBMers understand that most value comes from reaching prospective employees, business communities, and customers. Content is the context for the interaction. The structures of interactions vary according to the need and the situation, allowing teams to share social responsibilities. Regardless, employees are expected to keep social profiles current and manage other public spaces such as blogs on their own.

Social Initiatives

Connections drives social employee interaction within the brand as a by-product of IBM's commitment to social initiatives. The following programs drive culture and innovation within IBM and have led to some of the company's biggest breakthroughs in the past decade.

Jams

John Rooney informed us the Jams program first came into existence about 10 years ago. Jam events, held over the course of three days, are structured as threaded discussion forums to facilitate large-scale exchanging of information and ideas. These hands-on conversations are guided by a moderator who showcases key ideas. This is achieved by placing key ideas at the top of the thread in order to encourage participation, breadth, and depth.

The rating and voting systems built into the Jam interface allow participants to quickly gauge which ideas have the broadest support. Conversations can range from corporate strategy to issues of engagement. The Values Jam in 2003 gave employees the opportunity to redefine the brand's core values for the first time in almost 100 years.

The 2006 Innovation Jam, IBM's largest Jam to date, involved over 150,000 people representing 67 companies in over 100 countries. This Jam ended up producing ideas for 10 new IBM businesses, many of which evolved into the Smarter Planet initiative (see below), with seed investments of $100 million.[3]

Hack Days

The concept of hosting a "hack day" at a company didn't originate with IBM. Many smaller companies and start-ups began the practice roughly 10 years ago as a way to encourage innovation among the staff. At IBM, the idea for incorporating the practice began very socially. John Rooney shared with us that a few years ago an employee noticed a story on Yahoo! describing hack days at other companies. This employee was so intrigued by the concept that a blog was created and posted through Connections that argued in favor of experimenting with hack days.

The idea soon reached IBM executives, and the decision was made to move forward. Annual IBM Hack Days involve a few thousand employees who take breaks from daily duties to focus on specific challenges for the brand. Rooney says these hack days can be tailored to address anything from technology to a procedural "pain point" in an employee's work life. In the event that the hack isn't technical in nature, employees work to examine how changes can be made to embrace a spirit of social culture within a task or activity.

The Technology Adoption Program (TAP)

According to John Rooney, "We have a culture and history of innovation and engagement with employees. As we were embracing the web, we were seeing new technology coming from all corners of the company." However, with so many good ideas coming from so many different places, IBM had to come up with a way of collecting these new technologies into one place so the merits could be tested.

Enter the Technology Adoption Program (TAP), which was introduced as an early adoption, or "open-beta," program for employee volunteers. Through TAP, employees use new tools and provide direct feedback to the developer. As mentioned earlier in the chapter, the Connections platform arose directly from this process. Originally, the different applications that would come to be known as Connections began as separate ideas. However, once enough of the 140,000-plus employees in the TAP program saw the usefulness as a combined platform, the first version of Connections software was born.

To facilitate the TAP program, IBM hosts a website with a catalogue of new technologies in development. Participating employees are invited to select and test any of the new projects. After having used the product for a while, employees leave comments and suggestions for the developer. Through this process, TAP is able to host a variety of projects, from early tests for planned commercial products to plug-ins that employees designed for fun.

Forward Thinker Program

After completing the proper training, employees can nominate themselves to engage socially on behalf of IBM as part of the Forward Thinker Program. This system is designed to identify and empower the many subject experts—including several Nobel laureates and scientists—within the IBM ranks. These experts act on behalf of the brand as part of an interactive directory that matches them with potential customers and knowledge seekers. These programs foster brand eminence in the marketplace while helping company experts to emerge as valuable resources in the many markets and industries IBM caters to. By making the right tools and information available, IBM is changing the way its employees think about social business by weaving it into the company's culture.

IBM Select

The IBM Select team could easily be seen as the cream of the crop of the Forward Thinker Program. The group involves the brand's most valuable subject matter experts and uses social listening and analytics tools to try to develop a more advanced understanding of the social behaviors of their audiences and engage them with IBM experts.

Client Executive Engagement

Under this program, IBM uses Connections to set up a social B2B community to ensure that members are communicating and collaborating effectively with customers. The IBM team works directly with clients in an everyday capacity through the community in an easy-to-manage platform.

Mentoring

Social Selling Champions Program

When considering social initiatives, IBM must develop programs that are scalable for an international brand of over 400,000 employees and also be adaptable to specific regional needs. Jennifer Dubow acted as a "change agent" within the brand to help drive adoption of social selling as an essential part of employee culture. To accomplish this, she championed the Social Selling Champions Program. The program is designed to foster peer-to-peer learning through the concept of "change champion" networks. An IBM study showed that peer-to-peer networks are more conducive to learning about digital tools and social media than relying on one's managers.

Peers who are more experienced in establishing B2B connections through platforms like LinkedIn or Twitter volunteer their time to help serve as role models and mentors. These employees will work with approximately four other team members. Sharing advice and insights on best practice social selling strategies and showing the ropes of social media are general topics covered. Dubow noted important strategies are the sales associate's ability to connect with customers in social venues and the level of engagement with which they are comfortable.

Dubow said the primary purpose of the programs is to promote behavior change by modeling successful techniques of engagement. As an example, Dubow mentioned the challenge IBM faced when it first began rolling out personal sales rep pages for the employees. The pages were to include a brief blurb about the rep, contact information within the company, and how to reach the rep via social media. The pages also offered a text chatting tool to allow users to directly engage with social employees. Initially, many sales representatives were hesitant to set up the pages and were concerned about the additional requirements being placed upon them.

Dubow and her team wanted to help drive a behavior change so the sales reps would learn to accept and adopt new tools and selling practices. To overcome the initial resistance that many sales reps showed to the new way of selling, Dubow focused on activating employees around a peer-based mentoring system. Employees had the opportunity to engage and learn from each other directly. This proved to be an ideal solution to the problem.

Aside from providing training and positive role models, Social Selling Champions also receive leadership development and management training. This training furthers their skill set. Peers assigned to each group are monitored and advice is offered when necessary. As Dubow said:

> It is through influence, not authority, that they can coach their peers and show success stories. When people are resisting, you can't argue with emotion. And people resist for lots of reasons. With this program, what we want to do is model positive behavior and attitudes, and continue to share these stories so that those who resist can see they are missing out on achieving better sales results by not participating.

Social Buddy Program

This is a reverse-mentoring program and is designed to help get executives up to speed on social platforms and social media best practices. Through the Social Buddy Program, a sales rep is paired with an executive for one-on-one social media coaching sessions. During the coaching sessions, concepts like managing networks across multiple platforms and keeping social profiles up to date are discussed. Kelly Meade, a Cloud Sales Representative at IBM, stated the Social Buddy Program is just one part of the company's comprehensive list of mentoring programs.

Follow the Leader

Since social learning also requires social engagement, executives are tasked with putting their newfound skills to use in the Follow the Leader program. According to Sandy Carter, the program was designed to help push IBM managers and executives out into the digital space so brand values and practices could be modeled. Doing this helps set a positive example so others will follow. Carter set up social business coffee break videos, which offer short two- or three-minute clips that teach quick lessons about social business at IBM. The videos offer assistance and leadership to employee teams and potential clients, and have received an excess of 4 million views.

Blogging

To help facilitate the many types of content needed for an international brand with a leadership role in the B2B community, IBM developed many different blogging initiatives, each tackling a different as aspect of social business.

Smarter Planet

This content hub offers IBMers a chance to cultivate thought leadership on a variety of topics—from social media to healthcare, transportation to environmental sustainability. The goal is to spark engaged, intelligent, and respectful conversations around innovation in the spirit of seeking greater understanding. The blog represents community outreach on behalf of the brand, as it works to engage the world at large on topics that don't necessarily have easy answers.

Citizen IBM

Citizen IBM extends the spirit of the Smarter Planet blog by putting ideas into action. This site helps foster discussions surrounding specific IBM corporate citizenship programs, from education to volunteering. It also highlights the community-building efforts of individual IBMers, nongovernmental organizations (NGOs), and government officials.

IBM Research

This blog provides the public portal of the vast IBM Research unit. The Research team uses this platform to share developments in a variety of ways, whether sharing news or interviewing an IBM scientist. By focusing on the individual accomplishments of people and programs, the brand is able to put a very human face on a very large group of IBM innovators.

Midsize Insider

IBM thinks of the Midsize Insider as a valuable repository of expert content. It is tailored for small-to-midsized business owners and IT decision makers. The insights and tips on the blog come from experts who apply actionable business experiences. The experts help guide social-minded businesses toward methods of creating efficiencies and businesses delivering results.

Social Footprint

Through the combined efforts of Connections, social employee programs, and engaged blogging networks, IBM has built a modern enterprise on social engagement through industry-leading enterprise software and a culture of empowered content creators. The brand's Connections software enables seamless B2B interactions while simultaneously generating valuable insights through data analysis systems. Because of this, as IBM walks through the ever-changing digital village, it is leaving a large social footprint.

Since 2005, IBM has:

▶ 433,000 employees on IBM Connections
▶ 26,000 individual blogs
▶ 91,000 communities
▶ 623,000 files shared (and 9.5 million downloads)
▶ 62,000 wikis
▶ 50 million instant messages/day

Outside of Connections, the employees also have a firmly established presence:

▶ Facebook: more than 200,000 employees
▶ LinkedIn: more than 295,000 employees, with over 800,000 followers of the brand
▶ Twitter: more than 35,000 employees

Voices

In an effort to bring the authentic voices of IBM subject matter experts into the spotlight, in February 2013 IBM launched a social media site and web service called Voices. According to Ethan McCarty, this social aggregator "showcases live social feeds of IBMers who are experts in big data, mobile, social business, cloud, cognitive computing, and much more."[4] Employee blog, Twitter, and video feeds are supplemented by brand channels such as @SmarterPlanet and @IBM-Research. A word cloud at the top of the page shows trending topics in the IBM community.

This combination of both individual and official channels provides a complex view of the company, and perfectly embodies McCarty's "bag of marbles" concept with the surface area it produces. The variety of topics and channels—all anchored by authentic, engaged brand ambassadors—provides visitors with a depth of expertise that few, if any, brands can duplicate. As McCarty says, "Voices personifies IBM's values-led culture and massive social media footprint."[5] For critics who worry that social interaction can only lead to superficial engagement, this consolidation of content offers a powerful counterpoint.

McCarty certainly has big ideas for Voices, and can envision a day when aggregation pages like this one will replace "About Us" or "Community" pages on corporate websites. At its original launch in early February, Voices featured 150 different IBMers and channels, a number McCarty expects to increase tenfold by the end of 2013. Of course, more important than the number of contributors is the quality of content and the opportunity to build influence within the community. "On this new social playing field, the organizations that win will be those where employees can improve the culture by embodying their company's character to the world at large. . . . That's especially important for a business-to-business company such as mine."[6]

In other words, build character and integrity by offering transparency, authenticity, and expertise, and soon the results will come.

Key Takeaways

Dual Modes of Success

Ethan McCarty said that the social business must be able to operate along two separate trajectories: content and individual activation. Both have to be done right, but both must also be done individually. As McCarty said, "When you confuse the two, it leads to inauthentic outcomes. We've all seen videos that so obviously show that a company is trying to make a viral video. They don't work." Being able to produce engaging content may contribute to individual activation. To achieve this, the content must exist on its own merits and demonstrate value to employees or clients. If content is crafted to be useful instead of flashy, employees can establish the grounds for activation by demonstrating an eagerness to be helpful and engage others.

Influence Is Negotiable

Influencers both within and outside a brand have proven to be an interesting phenomenon: one minute they're the toast of the town, and the next minute they're yesterday's news. However, establishing relationships with other experts, whether internally or externally, is an important part of both B2B and social business best practices.

According to McCarty, while many companies take a panopticon-style approach to social media by constructing command centers, IBM federalizes this process as well. The social IBMer knows that an essential element of engagement is listening. Teams within the brand tend to be able to identify influencers, experts, and thought leaders through the normal course of their own social activities. This approach will allow the right people to organically develop the right relationships over time.

Walk the Talk

Jennifer Dubow said she often hears sales representatives comment on the importance of seeing their sales leaders on Twitter or LinkedIn. Public visibility demonstrates that these leaders are willing to walk the talk with social media. Dubow has even run coaching programs at IBM designed to help executives build strong profiles on public platforms. The simple act goes a long way in encouraging other employees to adopt social policies, update their own profiles, and utilize collaboration tools.

As John Rooney stated, deploying the technology is the easy part. The challenge is being able to align the tools with the culture of the company. Community members learn from each other, and employees understand when management is being authentic. Social employees cannot engage authentically unless they embrace the culture of transparency. By maintaining professional, regularly updated profiles, these employees model behaviors for other team members and set the stage for a culture of technology adoption.

Moving Forward

When we asked Ethan McCarty what the future might hold for IBM's social employee initiatives, he laughed and remarked, "We have our hands full!" Executives at the brand see no shortage of paths for the technology giant moving forward. However, McCarty indicated that one essential goal for IBM was to increase the visibility of the brand's social efforts.

After leading the B2B market for enterprise social software three years in a row, IBM is hoping to start showing its social presence in aggregate. IBM's strength comes from its rich interpretation of what it means to empower a culture of social employees. Vetted by TAP testers and integrated into the brand's own enterprise system, IBM's products reflect the very philosophies and processes that went into them. With a corporate culture dedicated to championing its employees' best ideas, IBM is certain to play a leading role in the future of social business.

CHAPTER 6

How Adobe Manages Social Media Using Guardrails

Software giant Adobe is perhaps best known for its industry standard programs like Photoshop®, Flash®, and Adobe Reader®. The company first became aware of the need to develop a companywide social media strategy in 2009 when it discovered disparate pockets of social media activity that had sprung up across the company among passionate employees. This decision was the next logical step for the brand. According to Maria Poveromo, Senior Director of Social Media and Public Relations at Adobe, the company was a social brand "before the term was coined," due to the close connection Adobe has always had to stakeholders, customers, and employees. Like many of the brands we spoke to, Adobe perceives itself as a social business because of the way social media is in the DNA of the company and is a major part of every department. Social media platforms aren't simply a means to an end shuffled into place to help the brand do business, they *are* the way the brand does business.

Adobe's philosophy extends beyond simple procedural considerations. Operating as a social business works only if each employee understands the value these programs bring to the brand. As Poveromo says, "It is part of a shared vision among executives and the employee base at large." Everyone has to buy in to the process, from the C-Suite to the front desk.

At Adobe, one particularly supportive executive advocate is Ann Lewnes, Senior Vice President and Chief Marketing Officer. She was instrumental in providing both the resources and the funding for the brand's new social program. Lewnes foresaw the need for an organized social program before many other companies, and made the decision to create a dedicated social media team in 2009 (see Figure 6.1). To achieve this, Lewnes championed the program both internally and externally. Internally, Lewnes emphasized the need for her organization and the broader company to think "social first" by encouraging that social media be a part of each function and its respective strategy. Externally, she evangelized Adobe's social media initiatives, driving greater visibility for Adobe's position as a leader in the social space.

Shortly after Adobe decided to build an organized social media program in 2009, one of the primary tasks was to collaborate with employees in order to develop high-functioning resources and support, as well as empower them to engage on social media channels without fear of repercussion. Executives at Adobe understood that they had to make sure that any new structure of communication and collaboration within the brand adhered to the brand's core values. This meant "placing the needs and voice of the customer at the core of strategy and execution."

Today's media-savvy consumers expect authentic, helpful interactions with their brands—regardless of the nature of the interaction or the type of media used. In order to keep the customer's voice the brand's top priority, Adobe knew social practices needed to be adopted that were better aligned to meet customer expectations. According to Poveromo:

> *Social provides a direct interaction with customers on a scale never before possible. Now every employee, regardless of how far removed they are from direct interactions, has the opportunity and ability to understand the impact they and the business are having on customers.*

Adobe approached the idea of structuring its social media program to empower socially active employee brand ambassadors around one central question: How does a brand empower employees to engage

Figure 6.1

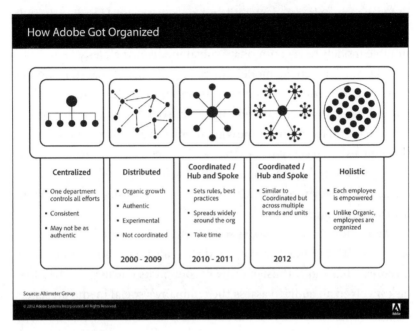

The continuing evolution of Adobe's organizational structure.

Credit: Adobe/Altimeter

communities independently through social media while keeping its brand identity uniform and intact?

The "Hub-and-Spoke" Model

Engaging colleagues and customers in the new digital bazaar meant Adobe had to organize its business around social media in a way that still maintained structure within the company. While exploring new social media organizational structures in 2009, Adobe came across the "hub-and-spoke" model, which had been highlighted in Altimeter Research findings and previously adopted at companies like Cisco (see Chapter 8). The general concept of the hub-and-spoke model was initially used in transportation by brands like Delta and FedEx as a way of coordinating ground and air operations. However, brands started to find new uses for the approach when they began seeking out suitable models to accommodate social media principles.

The hub-and-spoke model is made up of a set of shared resources that sit at the core of an organization and enables teams (spokes) around the company to better engage in social media. Such a model allows a brand to empower individual units to advance a brand's goals through a shared set of values, but without constant direct oversight. All teams are linked through this hub, offering employees a stable, universal platform for coordinating efforts and sharing important data and best practices.

According to Poveromo, as soon as Adobe identified the hub-and-spoke model, the brand recognized the cultural fit and opportunity it represented and enthusiastically set out on its journey. Adobe's first task involved an audit to assess the company's social media presence. Adobe executives then benchmarked these findings with those of other companies. Through this process, Adobe discovered that although the company itself had never issued any social media directives to its employees, the brand had pockets of well-established activity and innovation across the company. This included vibrant communities on Facebook and Twitter, as well as celebrity-like evangelists who were respected as credible sources of Adobe content.

As many other social brands have found, these independent early-adopters are very common in the workplace. By default, they have become the front lines of the movement toward a culture of social employees, although their motivation for adopting these new technologies is often much more pragmatic than revolutionary.

Unfortunately, as is often the case in loosely structured, largely improvised systems, Adobe also found "duplication of effort and a lack of knowledge sharing, and no protocols for escalating and managing crises." The company was proud of the innovation its employees demonstrated in addressing the rapidly changing media landscape, but it also saw that silos were forming around these groups of early adopters. Great strides in social collaboration were being made, but the innovations weren't being shared companywide, which limited the reach of potential improvements.

For example, various teams had already begun operating social media fan pages and Twitter accounts. However, each was a virtual island, cut off from both the brand and similar pages. Teams driving individual point products within Adobe's Creative Suite® line of products, such as the Photoshop® Facebook fan page or the Dreamweaver® Twitter account, were not connected to the teams driving the umbrella Creative Suite® Facebook page. Because of this, potential synergies in terms of content and programs were being lost.

Using the hub-and-spoke model as its starting point (see Figure 6.2), the brand began to devise an infrastructure and employee engagement system that empowered individuals to participate on social media sites in a more organized and strategic capacity, without risk of diluting the brand's mission or message. Through the establishment of regular meetings with dedicated social media leads across the company, content and best practices could be shared along with opinions on vendors, measurement practices, and upcoming initiatives with partnering opportunities for teams. Silos began to evaporate. The value of the new model was especially evident during the launch of Adobe Creative Suite® 5 in April 2010. Adobe employees were able to coordinate a major product launch across multiple product segments and time zones to successfully launch the Creative Suite® through a holistic social media strategy.

The Center of Excellence

At first, Adobe echoed one of the common concerns we addressed in Chapter 3: Won't there be consequences for giving so many individuals a voice in a brand's image? Of course, the reality is that employees are engaged in social media whether their activities are sanctioned by the company or not. For that reason, Adobe believed it stood in the brand's best interest to provide support and guidance to their

Figure 6.2

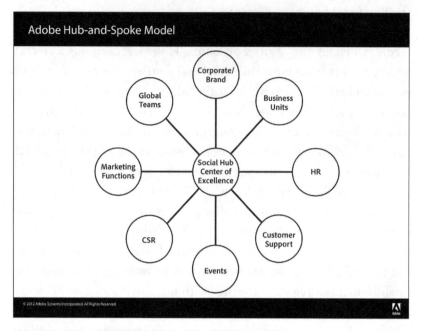

In Adobe's hub-and-spoke model, social business values radiate out from the center.

Credit: Adobe

activities by establishing a set of "guardrails" that would ensure all employees had access to a shared set of principles while retaining the freedom to engage in authentic interactions with customers or fellow employees. Adobe's Social Media Center of Excellence (CoE) came into being precisely to fill this need.

As Poveromo describes it, the CoE provides "a common framework and set of operating principles that empowers teams across the company to engage in social media in a more effective, strategic, and coordinated fashion." She credits Becky Brown at Intel for first coining the term "Center of Excellence," and cites Jeannette Gibson's masterful leadership of Cisco's own CoE for making it the success story that it is. To provide a steady mission and vision for the CoE, Adobe established four key pillars to guide all program decisions: enablement, empowerment, measurement, and innovation.

Enablement

According to Adobe, this pillar provides the building blocks or foundational skills for employees to engage. Through this process, employees gain a greater understanding of the value of social media in business through skill training, as well as best practice approaches to governance and crisis preparedness. "Our policies are actually a set of guidelines, or 'guardrails,' as we like to call them, that help employees understand the parameters of acceptable behavior when engaging on social media," says Poveromo. These guardrails include legal dos and don'ts. The following principles are examples of some of Adobe's guardrails:

▶ Do not post confidential information
▶ Add a disclaimer stating that views are your own and do not reflect those of Adobe
▶ Be authentic and truthful
▶ Always acknowledge and correct mistakes
▶ Engage with your audience by welcoming all opinions
▶ Do not defame or disparage others
▶ Use the established protocols to help address and triage common questions such as customer service inquiries

The guardrails approach may be a simple one, but it's incredibly effective and accounts for one of the fundamental realities of the social era. As Poveromo herself put it in an interview with Mashable, "Social media is largely uncharted territory and there are very few rules (it's too early to have experts)."[1] Further, it keeps things simple. Social engagement often occurs spontaneously and in real time. Because of this, social operating principles must be kept simple as well so the employee can respond quickly and confidently without having to consult an intimidating manual. It follows, then, that the simpler the guardrails are, the better. Adobe's core guidance in this regard is to use common sense and act responsibly. Says Poveromo, "We trust our employees to do the right thing, and they haven't let us down."

These foundational skills in the enablement program include basic, intermediate, and advanced-level trainings to ensure that employees and teams have the necessary engagement skills to properly represent their brand. "We also have a certification program, which consists of a thirty-minute basic training to ground everyone with common principles regardless of role or function," Poveromo says. To accommodate different learning styles, Adobe also provides self-training courses for many different social media platforms. To ensure convenience and easy access at any time of day, the company houses these courses on its intranet hub.

Adobe also offers training programs on a quarterly basis. The flexibility of the quarterly offerings allows Adobe employees to acquire social media skills at a pace that is comfortable to them. In addition, it allows employees to pursue the courses through individual motivation rather than from a sense of obligation. This generous program has been a hit with the employees, as well. "After three years of availability, we still see very high participation in our trainings each quarter," Poveromo said.

Empowerment

Once employees have mastered the basics of social engagement and become conversant in using different platforms, they begin to learn how to develop these skills beyond basic engagement in order to drive collaboration and innovation within the brand. CoE leaders advise teams on topics including how to improve their strategies and build programs that are robust and resourced adequately. The empowerment pillar also facilitates knowledge sharing by streamlining communications and providing forums for best practices sharing. Activities such as these allow the brand to communicate between groups spread across the globe. Adobe is so committed to getting social media right that it even opens its doors to other brands, social media vendors, and platforms like Facebook and Twitter. Through these presentations by external groups, Adobe's employees can gain perspective on the larger, industrywide conversation surrounding social media, and how their own work factors into it.

Measurement

"We are a company that strongly believes in the power of measurement—and, as such, we are rapidly becoming one of the first truly data-driven social media programs in the industry," Poveromo says. While measuring ROI in social media can be tricky—and as such is hotly debated—executives at Adobe believe they have found successful ways of measuring the brand's social media programs. In turn, this showcases the tremendous value of employee efforts.

The adoption of new business practices within an organization, whether social or otherwise, can often cause trepidation among employees. Adobe has standardized what it calls Key Performance Indicators (KPIs) that "ladder up to business objectives." According to Poveromo, "This common approach to measurement allows Adobe to prove the ROI of social media in terms of brand and conversion metrics." For an example of what these KPIs look like, see Figure 6.3.

Figure 6.3

Map Social Media KPIs to Business Objectives

BUSINESS OBJECTIVE	KPI 1	KPI 2	KPI 3	KPI 4	KPI 5
Awareness	Social Community Growth	Share of voice	Volume of conversations and reach	Ratio of positive, negative and neutral sentiment	Unique conversation contributors
Engagement	Percent of community interacting with content	Interactions per follower	Content virality and velocity	"Likes", re-tweets, shares, mentions, etc.	Campaign #hashtag use
Lead Generation	Cost per lead from social channels	RFI submissions through social	Qualified sales leads from social	Reach within target audience	# of white paper downloads
Demand Gen/ Conversion	Direct attribution - revenue & trial downloads through tracked links	Cost per acquisition	Conversion rates and average order value from social channels	Revenue attribution for key influencers	On-site product reviews influence on conversion rates
Customer Support	Cost savings (call deflection)	Avg. time to issue resolution	Change in sentiment around support issue	Number of issues resolved	Issue resolution rate per agent
Advocacy	Number of active advocates	Volume of conversations driven by advocates	Percent of brand communication driven by advocates	Influence score and reach of advocates	Revenue attributable to advocates
Product Innovation	Number of product ideas submitted	Number of ideas included in product development	Number of bugs reported and fixed	Size of community providing product feedback	Engagement rates in product forums

How Adobe uses Key Performance Indicators (KPIs) to achieve social business objectives.

Credit: Adobe

Innovation

As the title suggests, the Innovation pillar centers on the idea that brands can't afford to rest on their laurels in the digital bazaar. Instead, they must be constantly moving forward with new projects and experimenting with new social platforms. Perhaps most important to Adobe's bottom line, employees are also encouraged to implement pilot programs in order to drive business impact.

According to Poveromo in her Mashable interview, "Some of our more successful social media programs originated as pilots that teams were allowed to test."[2] The pilot programs Poveromo referenced represent a strong benefit of the hub-and-spoke model. Innovative ideas are able to originate from a decentralized source and grow on their own. If the idea or program proves successful during testing, it can be systematically distributed to the rest of the organization quite easily once it is presented to the central hub.

For example, when Adobe implemented Ratings and Reviews on its corporate website, the initiative began as a pilot. The team tested the impact of product reviews on a single product page. For their purposes, Adobe defined its conversion rate by dividing the number of purchasers by the number of visitors. For the test group exposed to the reviews pilot, Adobe experienced a 21 percent lift in conversion on the Photoshop® product description page and a 54 percent lift in conversion on the Photoshop® Extended product description page. This was in comparison to the page without reviews. Adobe also realized increased trials of both products when visitors saw reviews—13 percent and 35 percent, respectively.[3] Because of the positive results that the pilot yielded, Adobe was able to implement Ratings and Reviews for all of its flagship products worldwide.

Methods of Engagement

Finding the Stakeholders

Poveromo coordinates the brand's activities through the Corporate Social Media team, which—although it's nestled into the corporate communications wing of the organization—works to support social activities throughout the entire company worldwide. The scope of duties for this team is necessarily broad. As a result, Adobe had to develop a system that accommodated communication and engagement, but that did not require the team to micromanage every interaction. Adobe then adopted a policy of "influence without authority" in order to spread the brand's social message.

In order for this program to be successful, Adobe needed the support and cooperation of a number of teams and stakeholders. In every team or subgroup of employees lies at least one stakeholder. A stakeholder is a person who has taken a leadership role—either formally or informally—in order to develop social media practices in the group. These stakeholders are tremendous assets to social adoption, but only if they are included in the process from an early stage. Not only will the stakeholders know what kinds of tools would be best for their group to adopt, they will most likely have already taken steps to implement them.

This makes the stakeholder the first crucial intersection in translating a brand's mission on paper into a people-powered reality. If the stakeholder recognizes an opportunity to take a leadership role in social business projects, brands will encounter much less resistance in the implementation of the social employee program. These stakeholders will become employee advocates capable of spreading the brand's goals quickly and effectively throughout the company.

According to Poveromo, one of Adobe's early challenges was a lack of understanding from other teams about the CoE's charter and how the new organization would affect the social media work they were already doing. However, Adobe executives also knew their employees couldn't do social in a silo. A cross-department understanding of the brand's social mission and what was expected of each employee became crucial to the brand's success. Adobe was able to recognize the value of collaborating with individual groups in order to achieve companywide buy-in. Says Poveromo:

> Over the course of several weeks, we met with each team that we knew we would be working closely with. We explained our vision, addressed concerns, and asked for their insight.

Overall, the roadshow was very successful in helping to alleviate concerns, in building a sense of trust, and establishing a model of cross-functional collaboration. In addition, some of the early champions, including influential evangelists and bloggers, were concerned that we would mandate changes or limit their ability to post on social channels freely. Similarly, we met with these individuals to discuss concerns and to build cooperation. We also created a process to engage with these influencers in advance of big news or during times of crisis to discuss our strategy and enlist their help.

Another key aspect to note here is that the relationship with stakeholders continues beyond the design and implementation phase. Brands acknowledge that the social process remains an ongoing project. Social brands are constantly looking for new ways to improve their internal collaboration practices via social media. No program is developed overnight, and no company thinks it is "done" building a culture of social employees.

Brands like Adobe recognize that stakeholders are not only invaluable in the adoption phase, but also as living checkpoints for success essential to the operation of a social business. Although this issue may not be as pressing in smaller businesses, larger organizations identifying and collaborating with stakeholders find it absolutely essential. Larger brands simply don't have the resources to micromanage social adoption practices for an entire enterprise. "We had little to no authority over these teams to mandate change," Poveromo said. "So instead, we had to learn ways to encourage these stakeholders to see the value of working together."

Gamification

Employees should always feel there is some new objective to achieve in the social adoption process. One way to keep things fresh is by creating fun, opt-in-based objectives. Gamification can mean a variety of different things, from earning badges through social training programs to interactive approaches for raising brand awareness to getting employees involved in things like product launches. For instance, when Adobe launched the Creative Cloud® in the spring of 2012, the brand designed a scavenger hunt in San Francisco in order to encourage customer interest. According to Poveromo:

We needed employee volunteers to be stationed at each stop, and collected thirty employee volunteers with virtually no effort. These employees were not only willing to help—they took an active interest in understanding the best ways to engage with customers and had a great time doing it.

This example demonstrates how strong internal engagement spills out into the public domain. In the world of the social employee, the internal and external are inextricably linked. Although volunteering for a scavenger hunt certainly wasn't part of these employees' job descriptions, strong identification with the brand's mission and a desire to personally represent the brand turned promotion into a dynamic social gaming activity rather than "busy work." The event was a win-win for all parties involved. As a result of the engaging nature of the promotion, everyone involved became much more likely to share their scavenger hunting experiences within their own social networks.

Social Council

This aspect of Adobe's social program offers monthly calls to employees interested in learning more about best practices in social media. These calls include a wide variety of social branding experts from either internal or external sources. The council usually features guest speakers from other companies, as well as representatives from social media companies such as Twitter, Facebook, YouTube, and LinkedIn. The program has two natural benefits. First, it offers outside perspectives on social media practices, which better informs social employees and provides context for their own efforts within a larger conversation. Second, it makes implicit the brand's perspective that working with social media is an ongoing learning process, and not simply a "one-and-done" certification.

Content Calendars

A simple tool like a content calendar firmly demonstrates the "influence without authority" approach of the brand, and is designed to keep everyone apprised of larger company happenings in a nonintrusive way. Employees have access to a master content calendar through Acrobat.com that includes all of the brand's planned content for any given week. Employees are also provided with a weekly summary of content highlights, which they can use to share on their own channels. Finally, the Adobe Social® platform provides a companywide publishing and measurement tool that helps social practitioners schedule posts and tweets.

Distribution List

Adobe's social media team maintains a distribution list of over 2,000 employees whom the brand considers active in social media on behalf of the company. According to Poveromo, any time the brand has an event, campaign, or launch, these social media leads are encouraged to send an email to the distribution list (DL) with a summary of the content and sample tweets that employees can leverage. This process is especially striking for the amount of collective power it wields through small individual efforts. Through this process, social employees bring brand ambassadorship to a new level. They demonstrate to the public they are involved and passionate not only about their individual efforts within the company, but also about the brand's efforts as a whole.

Examples of Employee Engagement

In addition to the steady stream of content that is shared and used by Adobe's social strategists to engage with customers, another example is the ongoing work of Adobe's worldwide evangelist team.

This group actively participates on social media channels in order to better serve Adobe's customers. Evangelists travel regularly to conferences worldwide. Trainings and demos are conducted, which ultimately show the world how to create using Adobe technologies. This team always goes the extra mile by actively answering customer questions on various social networks, participating in Twitter chats, blogging frequently on Adobe news and information, and filming video tutorials on Adobe's products. The efforts of this team also illustrate that going social does not just mean engaging in cyberspace. These evangelists literally travel the globe with their message, ready to share with anyone willing to listen.

Another great example of how the company uses social media to engage with customers is Adobe's "Ask a Pro" sessions. The sessions are hosted each week by various product marketing managers, evangelists, and on occasion another customer. Topics are selected based on frequently asked questions and popular conversations that employees are seeing on social media channels. For example, if a good deal of chatter begins to build around a specific new product feature, an "Ask a Pro" session would be scheduled, and an expert on the topic would be available to answer any and all questions. To date, "Ask a Pro" sessions are one of Adobe's strongest and most popular social media programs.

Key Takeaways

Challenge the "Business as Usual" Mentality

The two things a brand should hold sacred in this time of upheaval are its basic values and mission statement. As long as a brand makes sure that all social processes are based on those principles, privilege should be given to the process that works best. If other innovations cause the process to become either irrelevant or inconvenient, a new process can be developed as a replacement.

Don't Boil the Ocean

Creating an engaged culture of social employees involves rethinking a brand's relationship to employees and customers alike. It is important for brands to begin building their social cultures; however, it is a long process and will not happen overnight. In this regard, smaller businesses will have the clear advantage when it comes to changing quickly. Ultimately, what matters most is that a brand does things the right way, not the fast way.

Adobe refers to this process as the "don't try to boil the ocean" mindset. As Poveromo says:

> *Plan your roadmap in terms of stages, so that you are making progress without trying to do everything at once. Patience is important, both in terms of allowing people to get on board and in terms of changing the way the company does things.*

Build Change Into the Process

A greater acceptance of change also emerges from the "don't boil the ocean" approach. As we said in Chapter 1, the very nature of change itself remains in constant flux. While brands should always have long-term goals in mind, flexibility in how to reach those goals should also be taken into consideration. "I'm pragmatic enough to understand that everything will change tomorrow. It's the nature of the social beast," Poveromo says. By focusing on small, reachable goals, brands will be able to constantly reevaluate the approach taken while working toward larger goals. If brands have to adjust course along the way, changes in approach can be handled without losing sight of long-term objectives.

Maintaining flexibility can also help bring a little extra clarity and perspective into the mix. A variety of new social platforms are emerging and offer employees new means of engagement, but not all platforms are created equal. In fact, many avenues will become dead ends. Adoption programs work best when focused on a select list of social projects. It is important to accept that boiling the ocean will only lead to confusion, disarray, and frustration—all resulting in a loss of time and money. As Poveromo says:

> At the rate that social media is moving and growing, it is impossible to stay on top of every new development. I think it's important that anyone working in social media filter through all the noise to find what works best for their company.

Let Progress Come Organically

We encourage any brand that adopts social business practices to stay active and informed of the latest developments, but that doesn't mean always jumping into every new opportunity headfirst. Each brand should find the internal and external platforms that are the best fit with the company's mission statement and needs. Exploring the possibilities within each system before expanding or moving on to other platforms should be a focus. Brands have the luxury of allowing the next steps of the process to be revealed organically. Allowing natural extensions of a current project to occur means employees will not waste time chasing "hot" new platforms down dead-end paths.

Taking the organic approach allows conversations about a brand's next steps to originate from within. This means the social operation of a brand remains focused on internal needs. External information, trends, and technology will then slowly filter in through early adopters. This filtration is helpful before recommendations are made to the community at large. Poveromo appears to trust this process implicitly as best practice for new program adoption. "I have the support of a talented staff and great consultants to keep me informed of developments. I learn from thought leaders in the industry and my peers at other companies who help me to isolate the signal from the noise."

Take a Multilateral Approach

Based on Adobe's experiences, Poveromo is convinced that brands must take both a "bottom's up" and a "top down" approach to organizational change. "Much of the change is grassroots, but it sure does help to have executive sponsors such as Ann Lewnes who share the vision of how social media can benefit customers and the company." In other words, employees may drive the change, but executive leadership can validate those efforts by providing employees with greater resources and introducing them to larger conversations about social media. As Poveromo says, "They can also empower teams to spend time on social media and reward innovative social media practices."

Brands Can Prove the ROI of Social Media

In summarizing where Adobe and the business world at large stand in terms of adopting social policies designed to empower the work of individual employees, Poveromo offered this assessment:

> While social media is in its early stages of evolution, it is also maturing rapidly and is increasingly expected to deliver business value. Metaphorically, it's growing up out of the awkward teenage years and now needs to get a job.

The company's Adobe Social® platform not only works as the common interface for social practitioners, but is also able to track social activities during major campaigns, launches, and events that directly lead to sales. According to Poveromo, during Adobe's launch of the Creative Cloud® in April 2012, the brand documented a tenfold ROI within two months.

It's Still Early

"The power of user generated content and distributed social networks to solve real-world problems is only beginning to be understood," Poveromo says. Adobe is incredibly proud of the work it has put into strengthening employee culture through social media policies and programs, but there is always room for improvement. Further explained by Poveromo:

Moving forward, our focus on social media will only increase. We will strive to be at the forefront of innovation and dedicated to the process of weaving employee, customer, partner, and stakeholder threads into one very humanistic communications tapestry.

Innovation is clearly essential to Adobe's continued goal of empowering its social employees. Social technology has essentially transformed the way we act both as employees and consumers. Benefits are not only delivered to businesses, but to the way brands and individuals are related to in the real world. Social business philosophies teach us this is a good thing. As Poveromo says, "Aligning social media goals with the brand, customers, and engaged employees can only benefit us all."

CHAPTER 7

How Dell Learned to SMaC-U into Social Success

The employees of Dell, Inc. have a long history of using the web as a strategic business tool. The brand was an early pioneer in e-commerce, first opening its doors to cyberspace in 1996. Even early on, the customer experience was central to the brand's philosophy, as evidenced by the first-of-its-kind program to allow customers to custom configure their own PCs online. Adopting the social web as a tool for doing better business has always been a natural fit for the brand, whether for assisting customers or for managing the company's supply chain and inventory.

To the employees at Dell, a social brand maintains social media as a core competency across the business and engages its customers online on a daily basis. Cory Edwards, Director of Social Media and Corporate Reputation at Dell, stated, "We're proud to be able to tick both of those boxes." Every employee at Dell understands that to be a social business, social media must be embedded in the very fabric of the company. To echo a common philosophy we heard among all the brands we interviewed, Dell understands that being a social business isn't simply about social media marketing or customer support. For over seven years since Dell first embraced the social business mindset, employees have learned to use social tools as they would email or a telephone. Social media is a natural extension of what the brand does, and employees at the company are confident that the tools available help them achieve better results both for their customers and for their business. Dell's success story examines the many methods employed in its B2B and B2C efforts, beginning with the organizational underpinnings that make the whole endeavor fire on all cylinders.

Early Adoption

Dell first became aware that critical consumer feedback was missing around 2005. Social media was still a relatively new idea at the time, but the brand realized that users were having their own conversations about the company via blogs, message boards, and other social outlets—and they weren't there to monitor or moderate any of it. Dell now estimates that as many as 25,000 conversations about the brand take place on any given day, whether positive or negative. Perhaps because of the brand's customer-focused experiences through the 1990s and into the turn of the century, executives at Dell understood the tremendous effect these conversations could have on the brand's reputation. Negative feedback can spread like wildfire across the social web, but it can also be extinguished just as quickly with the proper outreach programs. As a result, the brand decided to weave social processes directly into the fabric of the brand. As Cory Edwards stated, "We wanted to feel that customers were walking the hallways."

The idea of customers "walking the hallways" may have formed the most essential component of Dell's early social media adoption, but the brand also understood it wouldn't be able to produce the desired results without authentic engagement. Edwards felt the drive for authenticity was the primary driver for the brand's success:

> For us, it was about embedding social media into the fabric of the company and really empowering the employee to connect with customers. Since we started with that authenticity, it has allowed us to build a program with successful results. If the original goal had been focused merely on revenue generation, the program design and results would have been much different.

SMaC and SMaC-U

Michael Dell, founder and CEO of Dell, told us:

Engaging in honest, direct conversations with customers and stakeholders is a part of who we are, who we've always been. The social web amplifies our opportunity to listen and learn and invest ourselves in two-way dialogue, enabling us to become a better company with more to offer the people who depend on us.

With this in mind, the brand's ultimate goal with going social was to deepen customer relationships. Executives at the company understood quite well that they couldn't just command employees to "go social" and send them off on a mad scramble for the goal. Like many of the other brands we spoke with, Dell envisioned a comprehensive training program designed to help provide employees with the essential skills and tools needed to make social connections online. However, to make this program work, executives realized they needed early champions of the program, engaged workers who already had a leg up on their fellow employees in the digital bazaar.

Liz Bullock is Director of Social Media and Communities (SMaC). SMaC team leaders identified approximately 200 and asked them to take part in a social media pilot course for a program that would come to be known as SMaC University. According to Bullock:

Employees were involved in all the pilot classes for feedback. We felt that if they participated in these sessions it was a win-win to ensure our content was dead on, but also made sure they were aligned with our strategy and would share with other employees about the classes, as they had participated in the development.

After collecting feedback from the pilot group, the SMaC team was able to build a comprehensive training and certification program for Dell employees. Once all classes had been successfully built and perfected, the SMaC team launched an open-format "Unconference" to formally announce the launch of the SMaC-U certification program.

SMaC team leaders knew they needed to engage employees with comprehensive, hands-on content in order to convince them to activate around the program. Without engagement, the program would run the risk of being nothing more than a blip on the employees' radars, a brief reprieve from their daily tasks ineffective in driving behavior changes (see Figure 7.1).

In the eyes of most Dell employees, social media elicited a great deal of "personal versus professional" questions. Most employees were aware of the growing presence of social media in the public sphere, but they were unsure of what business applications these platforms would have—if any. This prompted the SMaC team to design highly interactive courses that involved real-world role-plays, case studies, and active discussions. The interactive nature of SMaC-U classes

Figure 7.1

Employees gather at Dell's Social Media & Community Unconference, July 26, 2011.

Credit: Dell

allows focus to center on teaching judgment above everything else. Bullock stated, "We felt the exercises would also give the employee confidence in what to do and not do, so there was more likelihood the employee would be active on behalf of the brand."

The SMaC team also wanted to make sure employees would continue to have conversations and learn about social business practices after their training was completed. To facilitate this conversation and ensure employees had the necessary resources to keep the conversation going, Dell set up a group through a Salesforce-designed platform called Chatter. Chatter offers employees an easy-to-use communication interface where teams can ask questions, share files, and manage project deadlines. This communication channel allows currently enrolled employees and SMaC-U graduates the opportunity to reinforce training by sharing experiences and questions with coworkers. While Dell has several different channels active at any given time, the SMaC University group boasts not only the largest enrollment (over 10,000 members) but also the most active community.

Certified in Talking SMaC

The level of employee interest in SMaC-U was much higher than the brand anticipated. While executives had hoped to train 1,000 employees in the span of about six months, they found the target number had not only been reached but had been exceeded after only one month. And the program hasn't shown any signs of slowing down since the initial push, either. Since SMaC-U's inception, over 12,000 employees have taken at least one course, with more than 7,000 employees achieving SMaC certification. According to Liz Bullock, enthusiasm for the program has been so great that employees have paid for their own travel to attend different trainings, and international employees have stayed up all hours of the night just to take certain courses.

One reason for SMaC-U's overwhelming success is it has received strong support from all levels of the company. While it is a given that social programs can't take flight until employees buy in to the initiative, both executives and managers must be active in the process in order to drive that adoption. The SMaC-U training program enables all employees to step up and be part of the conversation with Dell's customers and with each other. The program provides the opportunity to help amplify the many compelling Dell stories, engage proactively with customers, and show the many positive faces and personalities behind the Dell brand and technology. According to John Boyle, Senior Strategic Product Consultant & Digital Fulfillment Portfolio Manager, "Michael [Dell, CEO] is one of the most active and enthusiastic in the program. How cool is that?"

Dell's social programs thrive precisely because of the enthusiasm managers like Boyle bring to the table. Through the strong examples these leaders set, employees begin to understand and embrace social models of engagement. More importantly, however, they come to embrace the experience and see value in the new ways of doing things. One Dell employee's comments seem to summarize the general sentiment surrounding the SMaC-U program within the brand:

> I think social media training will aid me in having the proper tools to advise and engage the potential clients that I run across both locally and in international arenas. Dell's Social Media training helps prepare the associate to be on the cutting edge of this new process. I see nothing but positive benefits in having this training and certification.

Although Dell hopes to keep expanding employee engagement across social media, the brand also insists that all employees move through the necessary training channels first before acting as public social ambassadors of the brand. To accomplish this, Dell has created a set of certification requirements:

Mandatory Courses

1. *SMaC Principles:* This course teaches employees the brand's five core principles for proper engagement in the SMaC space:

a. *Protect information:* There is to be no sharing of confidential company information or customers' personally identifiable information.

b. *Be transparent and disclose:* When you talk about Dell on social media, it should disclose that you work for Dell. On Twitter, the brand uses hashtags (e.g., #iwork4dell) to clearly communicate this information.

c. *Follow the law*: Follow the Code of Conduct.

d. *Be responsible*: If something is seen being shared that is related to Dell on a social platform that shouldn't be happening, immediately inform the appropriate contact.

e. *Be nice*: Have fun and connect.

Dell also believes in publicly representing itself with consistency and transparency; therefore, the brand has also made its full social media policy available to the public online (www.dell.com /socialmediapolicy).

2. **Get Started SMaCing:** This course teaches how to strategically engage coworkers and customers through social media, and provides a set of tactics and tools to help take the guesswork out of the process.

3. **Building Brand on SMaC:** Through this course, employees learn how to help support the brand by producing and sharing content, using their voice, and acting proactively to help achieve the brand's goals.

4. **Platform Courses:** Dell employees are required to take a relationship-building course in one of the following social media platforms:

- Facebook
- Twitter
- Community
- LinkedIn
- Google+
- Sina (China)
- Renren (China)

Certification and Rewards

Once Dell employees complete SMaC-U coursework, a completion notification email is received when the SMaC requirements for certification have been met. Employees also receive a formal certification of their accomplishments. Dell employees report a great deal of pride in completing social coursework, and are proud to receive recognition for their efforts. According to Liz Bullock, "As we passed out certifications, we would start getting emails from employees if they didn't get their certificates in time."

The gratitude with which these certificates are received illustrates the value of rewards and recognition—and that doing so does not have to be an elaborate task. Being recognized for a job well done is often its own reward, and Dell employees are proud to flash their SMaC credentials in their email signatures or in the Dell Company Directory. However, Dell's social employees also receive tangible benefits as a result of their heightened status within the company. SMaC certified employees are granted access to the brand's publishing tools and can apply for Dell-branded social accounts.

Employee Unconferences

Dell also holds "unconferences" for its employees. These conferences are special open-format events held in the United States, United Kingdom, India, China, and Brazil. According to Bullock, events such as these are incredibly rare in a corporate environment. Despite their rarity, executives at Dell see these conferences as gifts that keep giving. Unconferences offer to employees both recognition for their hard work and opportunities to further expand their knowledge base.

During the conferences, more than 200 employees—from product engineers to marketing teams and corporate communications—are invited to learn about social media trends from outside experts. They receive reports on the status of Dell's own evolution using social media, and also participate in breakout sessions. Ideas generated during these conferences often become SMaC initiatives for the company, and those ideas that don't become informal tools in their own right by being disseminated through Dell's Chatter network (see Figure 7.2).

Figure 7.2

Guest participant Chris Barger examines an idea board at the Dell Social Media Unconference in Round Rock, Texas, July 28, 2010.

Credit: Dell

Get SMaRT

The SMaC team is a part of Dell's Marketing organization, and is responsible for driving Dell's overarching social media strategy, governance, tools, measurement, and training. However, it is not the brand's only team involved in social outreach programs. Dell's other core social media team, the Social Media and Reputation Team (SMaRT), is built into the brand's Communication organization. SMaRT focuses on programs related to influencers, reputation, and thought leadership—aspects that are a little more abstract in nature than those of the SMaC team. Both teams report to a director-level manager, with additional staff that operates laterally on a "dotted line" with the directors.

This system of interconnectivity allows employees to educate each other, share opinions and best practices, and ensure that the brand's mission is being upheld at all times. Because of this comprehensive system of education and communication, direct oversight is rarely necessary. As Edwards said, "We entrust our employees to do the right thing after being certified. If there is a misstep we are usually the first team to become aware of it and we will circle back and work with that employee to help them understand the guidelines."

SMaRT Initiatives

Customer Advisory Panel (CAP) Days

The Customer Advisory Panel Days program involves direct employee outreach to up to 20 Dell customers at a time who are actively talking about Dell online. CAP Days events are structured around open, honest, and collaborative dialogues in person. These are not simply cheerleading sessions for the brand. Both ranters and ravers from the customer base are invited into the discussion. This provides an opportunity for Dell to build relationships and learn from each other by bringing their collective communities and feedback together, as well as enjoying authentic, engaging conversation. Topics at CAP Days range from laptops to customer support to enterprise storage offerings.

The initial CAP Days event, held in Round Rock, Texas, in 2010, proved to be tremendously successful. Thirty customers participated in the first event, where Dell employees listened to first-hand feedback and showed off new products and improvements the brand was considering. The event created a considerable amount of buzz, garnering more than 128 million impressions on Twitter.

The brand also demonstrated its commitment to customers' contributions by flying the original group back to Round Rock a year later. The event exhibited the various ways Dell had applied customer feedback into its brand, its products, and its operations. This transparent engagement and accountability has proven a tremendous asset to the brand, and since then these CAP Day events have expanded out of the United States to Canada, Germany, the United Kingdom, and China (see Figure 7.3).

Figure 7.3

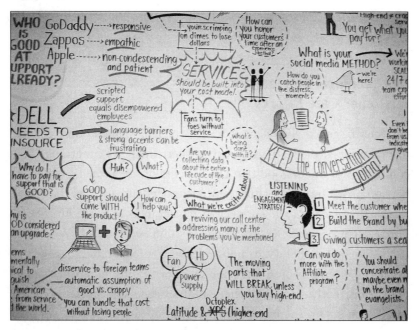

A Day 1 "Meeting Visualization" at Dell's first CAP Days event in Round Rock, Texas, June 15, 2010.

Credit: Dell

Social Think Tanks

The Social Think Tanks program grew directly out of the success of the CAP Days program, and is a prime example of the largely silo-free innovation enjoyed by social business models. In the Social Think Tanks, Dell subject matter experts engage with online influencers and other experts involved in particular industries or technologies— focusing on their challenges, opportunities, and future applications. This process provides a tremendous two-way exchange between Dell employees and industry experts. All participants collectively benefit from the shared knowledge and concerns put forth by members of the group.

These meetings are moderated by a neutral third party, and focus on topics such as healthcare, education, small business, cloud computing, and customer support. Through these diverse interactions, Dell employees are able to better understand the key priorities and needs of a potential customer base and build relationships with important influencers in a given industry.

Dell Technical Support and Customer Care Efforts

In order to scale their social media efforts, Dell understood it needed to make social media a core part of their business functions. The company also understood that the benefits of social media extended beyond providing support to their customers and allowed the brand to actually reach out and connect with customers in need. The Social Outreach Services (SOS) first began in 2006 as a sort of SWAT team headed up by Jason Duty. Employees would reach out to bloggers and other vocal online community members with tech support issues in order to directly—and publicly—address their concerns. By meeting customers on their home territories, the support team was able to remove most functional silos inhibiting effective support, and reported a 98 percent resolution rate.

The program continues to find new ways to either reach out or make itself available. On Twitter, the team uses the hashtag #DellSolves in order to build awareness of the outreach program. In May 2012, Dell employees under the @DellCares handle teamed up with YouTube to produce a series of "how to" videos to offer solutions to common technical problems. By providing this useful service to its customer base, the support team has also been able to devote more of its time to more urgent or nuanced problems.

Aside from boasting an astounding resolution rate, Dell has also found that this outreach program helps stem the tide of negative feedback rather dramatically. According to Cory Edwards, the SOS program has seen 42 percent of public "demoters" turn to "promoters" after the team intervened to help solve the issue. While ideally the brand would love to see this number climb up to 100 percent, the achievement is still highly significant.

As to the value of outreach programs such as these, one Dell employee said it best:

In marketing, it is often difficult to have interactions with customers, but if you don't spend time with customers, you don't really know what they are thinking. Social media gives me a front row seat to how our customers feel and what they think about our products.

SMaC Champions

Aside from this connections tool, the brand also employs several other groups that help keep employees informed, active, and engaged. There are over 7,000 SMaC-certified social employees at Dell. All enjoy a host of leadership programs that allow them to engage across the brand, the business community at large, and the company's customer base.

Within the group of SMaC certified employees, there is a self-selected subgroup called the SMaC Champions community. These elite employees are asked to fulfill activities for the company over the course of the year by putting their social training in action. After implementing this program, Dell executives were once again overwhelmed by the response. The brand had set the modest goal of 200 SMaC Champions involved in 50 activities through the 2013 fiscal year, but found they had exceeded that enrollment goal within the first 48 hours of announcing it. As of this writing, employee enrollment in the SMaC Champion program stood at over 500 applications for over 350 tasks to date.

These activities are all part of six key programs at the brand: driving listening culture, building connections with customers, internal expert engagement, event support, training/education, and community service.

Dell Rockstar Program

The Dell Rockstar Program ties directly back to Simon Mainwaring's argument that brands must become their customers' most vocal celebrants (see Chapter 2). The Dell Rockstar initiative identifies, engages, and empowers 75 Dell enthusiasts and advocates who share their expertise and passion with customers on forums such as the Dell Community. By giving special recognition to its biggest fans, Dell is able to tap into a prime resource for authenticity—thereby strengthening the brand/customer relationship in the process. Once Dell community managers have identified their Rockstars' areas of expertise, the Rockstars are then "married" to and connected with Dell experts in an effort to further drive connectivity and engagement between the company and its enthusiasts.

Active Listening

Dell has always considered itself to be a customer-centric organization, but Edwards admitted that prior to the brand adopting social business practices, the company's direct access to customers and customer insights had waned some. Executives at Dell quickly understood that social media had opened revolutionary possibilities in ways brands could communicate with customer bases. Company leaders moved forward to build outreach programs designed to bring the customer's voice into the center of the conversation, rather than keeping it on the periphery.

Employees at Dell don't just think that listening makes for good business; they consider it an essential pillar of social business. According to Edwards, "We continue to believe 'listening' and the related understanding and engagement with people is at the very root of our social business strategy." This means that listening must be purposeful, not passive. If the process can be likened to a day at the beach, brands can't simply be the tourists, eager to lie on their towels and hope to absorb the world around them. Rather, they must be the beachcombers armed with metal detectors and collection devices, tirelessly scouring the sands for every last bit of treasure—and eager to strike up conversations with any passing stranger willing to give them the time of day.

The beachcombers at Dell actively coordinate activities to strengthen listening programs. The types of content customers are most likely to engage with, and where they might go on the web to do so, are constantly evaluated. Determining the most holistic approaches to provide valuable content, it is clearly understood that engagement never ends, regardless of where a customer might be in the purchase cycle. Employees understand the value of follow-up actions, and know that customers and other stakeholders hold this aspect of communication in the highest regard. Dell beachcombers listen before acting, and are always ready to act.

The brand's social listening programs are multifaceted and diverse. These programs are anything but passive. In fact, many of Dell's innovative initiatives directly court customer participation—from brand advocates and detractors alike.

Social Employees Champion Compelling Results

Employees at Dell understand the value of making connections. Whether customers are commenting positively or negatively about the brand, Dell's presence on the social scene directly impacts the quality of discourse. According to Edwards, "In our early years of social media activities, engagement led to an almost immediate 30 percent decline in negative commentary in just a few short months." Building a strong online presence helps curb any negative publicity. The brand has also noted causality between social media activity and demand generation, as well as increased customer revenue. Dell has found that this process of engagement not only drives sales, but also customer loyalty through the relationships built online.

We had the opportunity to hear from a few employees at Dell, who were happy to share their experiences in Dell's listening program:

Employee #1:
A small Dell reseller was asking why a one-man shop couldn't be a Dell Partner certified on LinkedIn. We addressed his issue and moved the conversation to "How can Dell help grow your

channel business?" He is now one of our top promoters in our
Dell PartnerDirect group on LinkedIn.

Employee #2:

From the listen program, we found one of our customers was
looking for help with his PowerConnect device. But, he was
disappointed since everybody was talking about Cisco in [online]
communities. We found this customer, and Dell directly engaged
with him. He was so surprised and excited! He could not believe
the social community could help him talk directly to a Dell expert.
We changed this case from a story of disappointment to a good
customer.

Employee #3:

After listening to some customers who all had the same problem
with the same system, I was able to get a solution from our tech
support department and spread it to all of the customers, giving
a positive [customer experience] for Dell and making several of
our customers very happy with their systems.

The Social Media Listening Command Center

The rise of "big data"—a term used to describe the massive amount
of information generated through modern information-gathering
processes—has brought with it a very real logistical problem for
brands. Acquiring reliable consumer information and feedback is no
longer an obstacle, but now brands are often left wondering what to
do with the overabundance of data they receive.

In Dell's case, listening to over 25,000 conversations daily produced a wealth of data, but the brand has had to be creative in how
it sorts and utilizes this information. In 2010, Dell established the
Social Media Listening Command Center (SMLCC) led by Maribel Sierra. The brand has since designed over 300 monitoring categories in order to aggregate information by product line, customer
segments, and various business functions. The SMLCC is able to
sort data by criteria such as location/geography, basic demographics,
reach, sentiment, subject matter, and social platform.

Evaluation

To accomplish this kind of sorting, the SMLCC team uses Salesforce's Radian6 technology to assess and report on the trending social media topics related to Dell. The brand's focus on all details allows Dell to develop a complete picture of how it is viewed in the marketplace. This allows developers to better understand what products or company news is resonating with customers and how that information is being shared within their networks across the web.

Categorization itself isn't enough. Dell also uses additional natural language processing software and modeling analytics to make further sense of the tremendous amounts of data acquired. The end goal of these processes is to make the data more measurable and more meaningful as a tool to run the business. According to Maribel Sierra, this advanced processing software allows the brand to:

▶ Identify quality issues more quickly, enabling a more effective customer support response.
▶ Identify opportunities to share Dell IT solutions with IT customers who may be looking at various technology options.
▶ Associate and understand the root causes and issues that generate positive and negative sentiment.
▶ Identify and connect with people who may be having substantial impact on conversations due to personal knowledge and connections.
▶ Improve internal coordination efforts.
▶ Develop an early warning system.
▶ Streamline online response protocols.
▶ Set expectations and address misconceptions with customers.

IdeaStorm

According to ReadWrite Enterprise, "IdeaStorm is one of the touchstones of the enterprise social media age."[1] Launched in 2007, Dell's concept for IdeaStorm was to build a community site where anyone could submit ideas about improving Dell's products and services by allowing the community to vote for their favorite submissions. This blurring of roles allowed customers to directly participate in the brand's product development. In turn, this helped ensure that Dell's future contributions to the marketplace would be well received. Aside from the IdeaStorm web page itself, the team still currently operates the Twitter handle @IdeaStorm for easy customer access. To date, more than 18,000 ideas have been submitted to Dell through IdeaStorm and to date more than 500 ideas have been implemented through this program. A recent redesign of the IdeaStorm platform helps better support robust ideation, more prominent member presence, and better social sharing.

Dell employees involved in IdeaStorm actively engage in two-way dialogue with Dell's customer base. The IdeaStorm platform is also used to collect feedback on products still in the design and development stage—a process they call "Storm Sessions." The most successful of these events was the Project Sputnik Storm Session, which explored ways to integrate Dell's XPS 13 laptop with the Ubuntu Operating System in order to create a developer laptop. Within the first 24-hours of the session, over 40 ideas were generated. Not long after, over 90 ideas were on the table. The Project Sputnik laptop was made available to developers late in 2012.

Spreading the Word

Things said in public about a brand can affect every single member of the company. Dell circulates daily listening reports across the company, providing each employee access to feedback that directly impacts how they perform their jobs. The brand also circulates specific subject matter reports—generated either at the business unit level or through the brand's central Social Media Ground Control within the company's Social Media Command Center. This is done to help track commentary around acquisitions, product launches, hot issues, or new service and solution offerings. According to Edwards:

This kind of reporting drives deeper understanding of customers, our brand, and industry and technology trends, making social media a valuable way to connect with customers, as well as a tool to be deployed and used for research, analytics, and understanding more deeply our customers' experience.

Key Takeaways

Social Media Affects Every Aspect of Business

As Edwards stated:

After seven years of work in the field we have concluded that social media can impact every aspect of the customer experience and life cycle in positive ways, and in some respects, it also impacts the customer life cycle more than any other medium.

The importance of social media in the customer life cycle is apparent in everything Dell does. For this reason, the brand keeps its customer base front and center regardless of where individuals may be in the purchase cycle. In the brand's approach, we see our own model for the Möbius strip (see Chapter 2) perfectly reflected.

ROI Matters, but Doesn't Drive Social Media

Dell has been successful in justifying its transformation to social business practices through increased sales and greater customer esteem. Employees understand the bottom line is the fundamental motivator for social business practices but can't be measured in dollars alone. Dell's success story is driven by a customer-only approach, which begins with employee empowerment and radiates outward.

Dell measures this value not simply based on earnings, but on connections with new customers, building brand awareness, social advocacy, offering easily accessible support programs, and listening to and rewarding customer feedback

Little Changes Make Big Waves

Edwards admitted that, at first, Dell was somewhat hesitant about the idea of activating the entire employee workforce in the world of social media. Like many brands, Dell feared the ambiguity involved in such a move. Because of this fear, the Chief Marketing Officer,

Karen Quintos, was sought out for guidance. She was surprised to see an intriguing combination of employees who were hesitant about the SMaC-U program joining with employees who were extremely enthusiastic about moving forward. Employees were thrilled to receive the training, but were sometimes hesitant to jump into the social pool once training was complete. The solution to this problem turned out to be quite simple: give the employees clear objectives.

As stated in Chapter 3, going social is not an excuse for anarchy. Employees enjoy the feeling of empowerment, but the digital bazaar can be a nuanced and confusing place. It is for this reason that brand and individual interests are best served by creating clearly defined goals within the larger picture. Once a particular outreach program has been developed and mastered, the employee can move on to a new task. As Edwards says, this process makes it "less daunting for employees and it gets them to dip their toes in the social pool."

As an employee's experience in the social process builds, reservations start to dissipate. Dell has a newfound confidence in its employee base, which was bolstered by the brand's commitment to recognizing and rewarding "the fearless folks who started first." Teaching judgment and grounding all social practices in a comprehensive policy yielded employees who eventually became very comfortable with the movement through the social space. Dell felt these results in every corner of its business.

There was one comment Edwards made that especially struck a chord with us: "We see individual employees having direct conversations online with our most senior executives, when historically this wasn't always an option. Teams seem excited and more customer focused." Before the advent of social business, the thought of individual employees in a large corporation having direct access to the C-level was unheard of, yet it makes for a fascinating benchmark of the kinds of changes that a culture of engaged social employees produces. Just as a pebble dropped in a pond creates a much greater ripple effect, a small anecdote can demonstrate how cultural indicators have the potential to produce dramatically different results for customers.

CHAPTER 8

How Cisco Built a Powerful Employee Network

Cisco has a somewhat unique place on our roster of case studies, considering that the company has been in the business of connecting employees through integrated systems and networks from the very beginning of its existence. Social is very much in the company's DNA. In the early 1980s, the company's founders, husband and wife Len Bosack and Sandy Lerner, found they could not share emails with each other from their respective buildings on the Stanford University campus. Though the two worked in relatively close proximity to each other at the same organization, networked systems in the early 1980s still had a lot of bugs to work out. As the company says on its website, "A technology had to be invented to deal with disparate local area protocols; and as a result of solving their challenge—the multi-protocol router was born."[1]

One could say that Cisco was in the business of taking the world social before the concept was even a blip on the radar in business communities. The story of the company's inception also reveals an essential truth about the *why* of social business: it's not about what new technologies and gadgets a company can bring to the world, but rather about how those innovations are used to better assist interpersonal communication and engagement between employees. Bosack and Lerner wanted to improve their ability to communicate, so they built a product that would do exactly that. Cisco has quite literally made connecting people its business. Of course, the precise nature of the networking industry has changed considerably over the years.

Always Evolving

We interviewed Ron Ricci, Vice President of Executive and Customer Engagement, and Jeremy Hartman, Director of Applied Thought Leadership at Cisco. Our goal was to develop a better idea of what social business has meant to the company over the years, and how their groundbreaking approaches to social empowerment have dramatically transformed the organizational structure of the business in a very short amount of time. As stated by Ricci:

> Like all growing organizations, Cisco had gone through its phases of evolution. Cisco had a start-up product phase in the 1980s when the idea of networking computer and peripherals was born. The 1990s saw the build-out of the Internet, largely on Cisco equipment, which created tremendous growth as the company exited the decade with more than $20 billion in sales. The last ten years focused on integration across the company as customers asked for (and demanded) architectures instead of point products.

Ricci's observation regarding customer demand for architectures is especially telling, and it reflects a theme Cisco found again and again during the company's transformation in 2012. The challenge in the world of social business has become not a question of what tools to use, but how these tools can be effectively leveraged to enable an adaptable business architecture built around more open and highly flexible communication channels.

Cisco had played an integral role in bringing new networking technologies to the business world over the past three decades, and part of its brand narrative is the company's own use of networking technologies to run its business. As the company's position with customers evolved and new competitors emerged, executives at the company began to realize that the internal architecture of their own company was starting to show its age, so to speak, and needed to be upgraded to meet the demands of the social era. The company's wake-up call came in the form of its Fiscal Year 2011 Q1 results where revenues fell $500 million below the forecast. Wall Street's reaction was swift and employees at the company were surprised. From the C-Suite to the 3,500 members of the company's Strategic Leadership Community (SLC) and down to the rest of the company's 65,000 employees, the results put the company under a microscope and shook the confidence of its leadership team. "First of all, our view on this guidance is we're disappointed," said John T. Chambers, Chairman and CEO of Cisco, during the Cisco Q1 2011 Earnings Call. "This is something that if we were to look back just a quarter ago, we expected it to be in the mid-teens or higher and that's what I think our growth rates should be. If you look, we've got a couple of air pockets that we hit."

Turning Right

As Ricci explains, "The 'air pocket' put to test a culture that had long encouraged open communication, transparency, and executive accessibility." Executives and employees alike were proud of their corporate culture and the interactions it afforded, yet the downturn in the company's performance indicated that some substantial inefficiencies existed in how Cisco operated as a business. Communication and execution were breaking down at certain points in the chain, but no one could pinpoint precisely where or how. Compounding it all were the changing demands of the market: Cisco's customers needed the company to redirect its energies. The strength of Cisco's corporate culture had allowed the company to push through similar situations in the past. According to Ron Ricci, "The company has a history of successfully 'turning right'—as CEO John Chambers calls it—those extraordinary moments where passion and belief create discretionary effort in pursuit of an important mission." The company had leveraged this strength in its internal culture on many occasions throughout the years to encourage members of Cisco's leadership team to quickly buy into organizational changes—sometimes unpleasant changes—necessary to adapt to changes in the market.

That latest incident, however, proved to be a more challenging task. Jeremy Hartman said:

> In truth the company needed to turn right on several fronts. Most importantly, we had to switch from thinking of ourselves as a products and services business to a solutions business. This was a huge shift for the company, and we realized to be successful we had to rethink how we aligned our leaders to the priorities and decisions of the company. Ultimately, this necessitated putting in place a social-based communication model to drive engagement on a completely new level.

One concern the company faced was figuring out how to expedite the transition. The executives at Cisco felt they had to simplify the company's operating model and organizational infrastructure to accelerate the shift to a services and solutions model. However, they also knew that their customers and stockholders expected results. Internal restructuring may have been the most important aspect of the transition, but, as Hartman pointed out, "It's the results that restructuring produce, not the restructuring itself, that the outside world cares about." Because of this reality and the company's desire to quickly regain market share, leadership decided to execute a transformation plan that had many different "right turns" for the company— all of which needed to be done simultaneously.

First Step: Regain Confidence

"The complexity of executing Cisco's strategy simply became, well, too complex," Ron Ricci said. "As Cisco moved beyond core markets of routing and switching, navigating the decision-making process inside the company became increasingly difficult." Ricci likened the challenges in the decision-making process to "gunk" in a system. "Gunk leads to friction, and friction slows execution, and slower execution deflates discretionary effort." As the company would come to find out over the course of the following year, the hang-ups in decision making stemmed directly from the ambiguous decision rights on the leadership team—who decided why something was important, and what made something a priority? More concerning than that ambiguity, however, was the noticeable lack of buy-in among the members of the leadership team to what Cisco was trying to do.

When longtime Cisco veteran Gary Moore became the company's first Chief Operating Officer in February 2011, one of his biggest priorities was to regain the SLC's confidence in the company, its decision-making process, its values, and its priorities. As Ricci put it, "If the SLC wasn't fully bought in, Moore knew the future of Cisco was at stake." Fortunately, Moore and CEO John Chambers recognized the perfect platform for engaging the SLC.

The Strategic Leader Exchange

For 15 years, Cisco had held an event called the Strategic Leader Offsite, a gathering of the SLC designed to help the company set the agenda for the coming fiscal year. Beginning in 2008, however, Cisco had begun to restructure the event around some of its existing digital technologies such as Telepresence and WebEx in order to reduce travel expenses. By 2012, what was formerly a two-day event had gone completely virtual and was rebranded as the Strategic Leader Exchange (SLX). This change turned out to be incredibly fortuitous for the company. "What started as a way to save money evolved unexpectedly into a completely new way to engage leaders to collapse time-to-action," Ricci said.

Cisco's agenda for the 2012 fiscal year was incredibly ambitious, to say the least. According to Ricci, "The priorities included the most significant internal transformation in the company's history, a dramatic effort to simplify how the company worked, and refocus the company on its core markets." However, at the beginning of the fiscal year in August 2011, the path toward these changes remained somewhat unclear. "No one knew it at the time, but important organizational changes and long-held assumptions about the way work would get done were only months away."

Challenges at Every Step

Logistically speaking, Cisco faced several very important hurdles. The first was the nature of the organizational restructuring. In order to coordinate a discussion between the 3,500 members of the SLC in conjunction with the company's executives, Moore and Chambers had to be sensitive to the very real knowledge gaps at play between the individuals and the functions they represented. Further compounding the situation were nondisclosure issues that prohibited a linear exchange. "The requirements for success turned the SLX platform upside down," Ricci said. "It had to be as nonlinear as possible in execution and be able to close specific gaps of information on complex topics."

The technology to facilitate the SLX events wasn't an issue; the real issue was the need for a process that would create a rich, open dialogue and an environment where "lumpy" levels of information existed across the different groups. "We needed ears everywhere," Ricci said, "especially to avoid headquarters syndrome." Much to its surprise, the company discovered that some of the simplest tools at their disposal were the most effective: tools such as instant messaging, chatting, and texting combined with global video conferencing capabilities across desktops, tablets, and mobile devices. In designing this SLX, the Cisco team integrated these tools directly into an engagement process. "We weren't trying to change the tools people loved— like chatting—we needed to put them into an active-listening process where they worked to solve the listening-knowledge gap we had," said Ricci. Through a remarkably innovative structure for exchange, suddenly 3,500 individuals would be able to speak simultaneously as individuals and as a collective voice.

Multilevel Monitoring

Because of the needs for a dynamic yet inclusive conversation, the Cisco team devised a multichannel approach that would allow the conversation to progress on several fronts simultaneously without causing any lags in the exchange. Cisco had always had a reputation for open dialogue and employee empowerment, but the company was adamant that the SLX conversations take that engagement to new levels of authenticity. "We wanted the audience to effectively steer the conversation in real time to what mattered most in understanding the transformation," said Ricci. Moore and Chambers knew that SLC buy-in to the internal revamping of the company was essential for the change to take hold in the most efficient manner possible.

To accomplish that, the Cisco team designed the active listening process around four key capabilities, all operating simultaneously for any SLX production. Further, the conversations that would be taking place had dynamic needs; therefore, the listening process couldn't be automated. The Cisco team had to synthesize hundreds of inputs in real time to make sure they weren't missing any trends in the conversation. Ricci and the monitoring team felt it essential to maintain such a high level of vigilance, as "it is easy to miss the forest for the trees in the heat of the moment."

Although the four-tiered system sounds complicated and distracting, Ricci and his team found that the four-tiered system worked like "engagement on caffeine," facilitating conversations in a rich, dynamic way. The four channels are described here.

Real-Time Broadcast Channel

This channel allowed information to flow bidirectionally between the "audience," or the SLC leaders, and the speakers. This platform served as the primary exchange hub for the discussions. Because the team valued genuine, unscripted responses to issues and questions, they set up a process where they could deliver important information to the Broadcast Channel without any forewarning.

The team set up a war room with the explicit purpose of issuing "trend alerts"—those times during the sessions when pent-up audience discussion in the chat room needed addressing during the live sessions. These trend alerts were issued from the war room without any advance notice to the executives participating in the sessions. The alerts were sent directly into the broadcast production so the leaders online understood the moderators were acting in response to the leaders' energies. Says Ricci, "The value of representing the leaders authentically—without any notice—cannot be underestimated in the credibility it created."

Question Manager Channel

The Question Manager Channel (see Figure 8.1) allowed members of the SLC to submit questions anonymously to a group of executives.

Figure 8.1

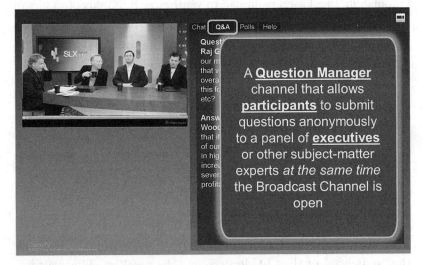

Credit: Cisco

The executives would receive these questions while the larger conversation in the Broadcast Channel continued, and would help steer the conversation toward the most pressing matters. These questions would usually be in response to the larger conversation on the Broadcast Channel. Allowing anonymity on this tier gave members of the SLC the opportunity to pose direct questions to the executive team without having to compete with noise from the larger conversation in the Broadcast Channel.

Peer-to-Peer Channel

The Peer-to-Peer Channel (see Figure 8.2) allowed SLC members to discuss issues or challenge assumptions among themselves during the broadcast. This tier was essential to the exchange, as it provided leaders the opportunity to coordinate their thinking and seek better understanding with one another. By giving the leaders a channel in which they were protected from executive oversight, the leaders were able to sort out concerns and prioritize questions without slowing down the larger conversation.

Figure 8.2

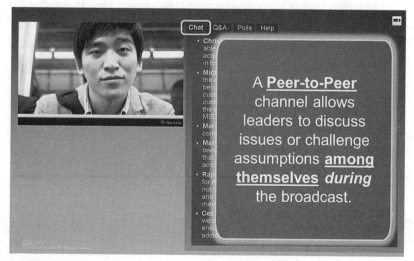

A **Peer-to-Peer** channel allows leaders to discuss issues or challenge assumptions **among themselves** *during* the broadcast.

Credit: Cisco

Polling Channel

The Polling Channel allowed the group at large to capture input on certain topics quickly and efficiently. This channel proved to be invaluable in measuring the group's real-time thoughts on key issues, free of background noise.

Authenticity in Real Time

In Ricci's opinion, the value in this approach rested in the ability of the SLC team to "see" that they were being heard. By filtering input from the Peer-to-Peer and Polling channels directly in the Broadcast Channel at opportune moments, leaders were able to see that not only was their input being monitored and quantified, it was driving the conversation. Entire conversations could be adjusted and redirected based on polling input. For instance, if results showed that a large percentage of the SLC team had lingering questions on a particular subject, the group would then give precedence to that subject until everyone was back on the same page.

"The fact that it was obvious and transparent that the audience was guiding the conversation energized the authenticity of the conversation," Ricci says. "It goes without saying that the Cisco executives in these sessions deserve quite a bit of credit; talking to thousands of leaders without knowing the questions during a time of significant change—changes not everybody agreed with—takes confidence and courage." But more importantly, this willingness to be put on the spot and share in an earnest exchange with their leadership team showed that the executives were more than willing to put their money where their mouth was. This transparency showed a tremendous deal of individual accountability, which in turn lent both credibility and a sense of good-faith urgency to the whole endeavor.

WWHW

The SLX sessions stretched out over a period of six months from December 2011 to May 2012. The exchange involved over a dozen sessions. Some sessions were as short as an hour, while others lasted as many as two days. While Cisco's executives were certain that these authentic exchanges were increasing engagement from the SLC team, they still had to be sure the conversation was moving forward at a pace sufficient for the company to meet its transformative goals. Hartman and his team could sense in real time that the leadership team was moving down the change curve, but they wanted to be able to put hard data behind what they were observing in the listening process. Said Hartman:

> It happened somewhat by accident, but we built a research instrument based on the way leaders were talking to us in the listening process. These leaders kept asking the same basic questions: What *are we doing?* Why *are we doing it?* How *is it getting done?* When *do you want it done? It was a natural progression of change in simple language that was theirs.*

Resisting the temptation to overthink the dynamic they were observing, the team built a research model that they affectionately named the "WWHW Wheel." This research model measured individual, functional, and geographic standing against the What-Why-How-When progression of understanding around Cisco's transformation.

The spontaneity of this innovation, as well as its simple-yet-pragmatic approach to a key question, represented a key aspect of social employee culture. By allowing employees to have direct input into the company's transformation process, Cisco could devise a matrix that would directly aid in the conversation. The WWHW Wheel provided a quick and accurate gauge of where the management team was, and how prepared members were to buy in to certain aspects of the transformation process (see Figure 8.3).

The early stages of the wheel, the *what* and the *why*, generally indicated that the SLC was still trying to grasp some of the changes the company had planned for the future. This is not to say that the team was responding negatively to these proposed changes, just that they were still in the process of integrating the concepts into the architecture of their own day-to-day responsibilities. Regardless, the first two stages marked the most crucial aspects of the wheel when it came to buy-in; if the SLC team couldn't reconcile the *why* of the change, then they would be hesitant to move toward actually implementing the changes (the *how*). Ricci stated:

> *In six months, the Cisco leadership team had effectively moved two big steps down the change curve. The research on the WWHW Wheel showed Cisco's management team had passed*

Figure 8.3

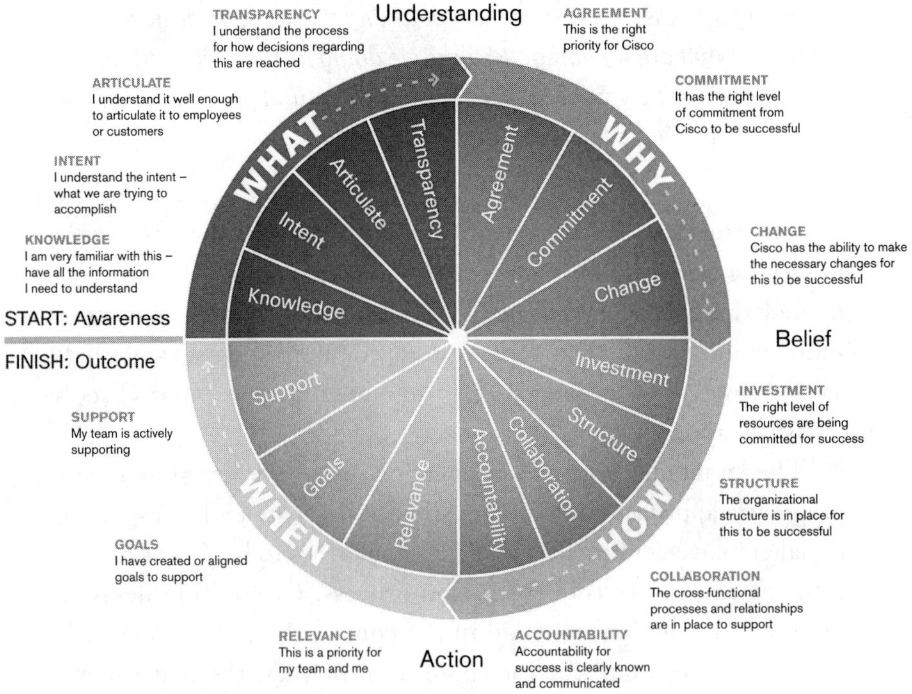

The WWHW Wheel: Cisco leaders build employee buy-in by guiding conversations through these phases of change and adoption.

beyond asking what and why to questions about the transforma-
tion, and were ready for action.

In other words, the SLC was ready to "turn right."

"Old School" Advocacy

Like many of the executives at Cisco, Jeremy Hartman was surprised
at how quickly SLC members became advocates of the company's
new direction once they'd moved past the *why* of the changes. As the
SLX continued to hash out the *how*, the 3,500 SLC leaders quickly
worked to spread the word to the company's remaining 50,000-plus
employees. Hartman stated:

> *It became very old-school. While technology played a huge role*
> *in aligning the SLC, once we got them engaged, the engagement*
> *became much more decentralized and personal. The SLC became*
> *feet-on-the street advocates, meeting with their teams in person*
> *in their own geographies.*

Cisco's approach to the SLX highlights the continued importance of executive leadership in social business. While the majority
of employees bought in to the company's restructuring plan through
organic conversation and advocacy as the SLX progressed, Cisco's
executives provided the vision. Further, they put their money where
their mouths were once again. The stunning transformation at Cisco
didn't just happen as a result of some monolithic directive from on
high. Instead, company executives invested themselves into the buy-in
process, relentlessly engaging in rigorous, multileveled conversations
with SLC leaders until they could secure unwavering commitment
from their management teams. "We decided alignment was very
important to the company moving forward," Hartman said. "We
knew that if we could establish trust in the individual directors, they
would become perfect advocates for these changes, and that their
teams would follow them."

Key Takeaways

Cleaning Up the "Gunk" by Defining Roles

Cisco prided itself on its collaborative skills and the "operational agility" this approach provided. However, the company found that this alone wasn't enough. "There were many aspects of the collaboration system that were not finished—and their absence created complexity and friction that slowed Cisco's execution," said Ricci. One problem businesses often face as they move to structures that favor organic input over hierarchical considerations is the apparent loss of decision makers. The company quickly came to realize that not only were decision rights ambiguous, but the company's larger operating model also lacked clarity. As Ricci put it, "It was easy to confuse 'urgent' decisions with important decisions. To the SLC, there were too many things to pay attention to and too many handshakes to make." To address this ambiguity and clean up the "gunk" that was slowing down business operations, Cisco developed the following guidelines:

- ▶ **Decision rights:** Tell people in your organization who gets to make decisions.
- ▶ **Focus on facts:** Communicate the financial and economic boundaries of decisions, and where data are sourced.
- ▶ **Taxonomy:** Make it clear what all the terms of your business mean.
- ▶ **Common vocabulary:** Ensure that decisions are defined and communicated in a consistent way.
- ▶ **Tell people how you make decisions:** Not everyone thinks the same way, and the more your peers know how you make decisions, the faster they'll understand you.

The "Why" Comes First

Cisco discovered through their many conversations during the SLX that engagement depends on answering the essential questions first.

Knowing the reasons why a certain task is important may not seem like a significant motivator, and it may not even seem very difficult to explain, but as Ricci stated, "When people hear about decisions, it's a natural human tendency to be curious. Unfortunately a person's questions often get left unanswered."

As we touched on in Chapter 2, a company's purpose is everything. It drives motivation, understanding, and urgency. Ricci stated:

> In our experience, alignment is all about what a team needs to prioritize. Engagement is about answering why something is important to prioritize, how you are asking teams to execute against those priorities, and when you need them to act.

Satisfying an employee's curiosity can sometimes be a tricky venture, but it is not an impossible one.

The most crucial step to the process involves an alignment and investment in strategy from executive leadership. This was demonstrated in Cisco's SLX initiative. The company's executives had to show a certain willingness to answer questions. "When communicating to leaders, our experience taught us there is a big difference between what and why," Ricci said. When a team is focused on the *what* of an issue, team members ask questions regarding responsibility. Who made the decision, who is accountable, and how credible is the accountability system? Such an approach will complete a task; however, the driving motivation will be on the structure of responsibility surrounding the project instead of on the project itself. This approach runs counter to the spirit of the social employee, who expects to be engaged by the tasks performed.

Changing the nature of engagement to one of *why* focuses the conversation on much more concrete justifications for a project. How was this decision approached, what facts or data were used in the decision, and what trade-offs were considered? These types of questions get to the heart of a decision, and the answers will demonstrate the amount of thought and energy already invested in the project, as well as why it matters. As Ricci stated, "Endless curiosity and second guessing is the enemy and slows you down. Passion comes from the exact opposite—not knowing what to do, but believing it is the right thing to do."

If employees can see how invested the architects of a plan were, they will be far more willing to invest themselves in the project as well.

Measure Engagement

Not every company uses the same approach to gauge the level of employee engagement. It's important for companies large and small to remember that it's not an impossible task. For the most part, simply asking whether an employee is engaged likely won't produce very useful answers, but engagement can be measured in the nature of a group's responses. Where are the employees trying to steer the conversation, what common issues are they raising? Do they appear impatient, or eager to press on? "We found out accidentally that there is a very effective way to measure the success of our message," Ricci says. During a session focusing on the transformational efforts in engineering, the SLX team began by focusing on the why questions of the transformation. As it turned out, however, the SLC felt they had already reconciled these issues and wanted to move on. Ricci says:

> Suddenly, during the session, the chat room chatter was sending us messages like "Why are you asking why we are doing this?" "We want to know how this is going to work." Social media is such a powerful sensing tool if you have the right processes and tools in place to take action. Right there before our eyes, members of the SLC were piling on that we were getting the conversation wrong. A change had happened. People had moved down the change progression.

Social Takes Time

As Jeremy Hartman says, "Social media wasn't designed for companies. It was designed for people." What may be quite simple in person-to-person communication via social media becomes increasingly more complex when more people are added to the conversation. While executives at Cisco are very excited about the role their business has been taking since late 2011, Hartman admitted that it hasn't always been easy for the company to adapt its internal structure in a way that gives greater agency to its employees. However, he said the company is excited about its social prospects moving forward and that Cisco's breakthroughs in communications strategies through the SLX has taught them how to use to social media internally, which makes communication with customers better.

In the span of a little more than a year, Cisco's shift from a products and services model to a solutions-based model has already brought the company clear benefits. The gunk slowing the decision-making process has largely been cleared, and employees at all levels now benefit from a more clearly delineated decision-making structure and stronger methods of engagement. To Hartman, a major factor in the company's success with social employee engagement stemmed from identifying a very specific need:

> Customers are scrambling to find the most out of the many different technologies available on the market. They're all saying, "We love the technology, but how do we get the most out of it?" This, itself, is a combination of process, culture, and technology. But you have to be specific with your goals to make it all work. The reason we focused on SLX is that it solved such a huge deficit for the company that other technologies and processes couldn't do for us.

The company has taken the lessons learned from the SLX and has applied them toward external engagement. Hartman said the company is very happy with the blogging program that has been put in place. Even this simple tool, he said, has made communication with important influencers and thought leaders much simpler, and much more informal. Here again, Hartman stressed that blogging is just a tool for exchange, and that the people, culture, and processes matter the most.

The People Drive the Process

Ron Ricci echoed Hartman's assertion. "The big lesson here isn't the technology, it is the process we built to listen and hear feedback in context to the What/Why/How/When change curve." This type of mindset underscores the transformative power of social business. Technology may have transformed the workplace over the past 30 years, but it's the social connections the changes foster that really drive organizational innovation. Further, connections can be monitored, measured, and leveraged to create powerful results for a company, all while increasing transparency and authenticity. With a business as large as Cisco's, institutional change can often be quite painstaking and stretch out over several years. However, by the end of the 2012 fiscal year, the hard work involved during the SLX program had paid off, and the company was ready to move forward. As John Chambers said during Cisco's Q4 2012 Earnings Call:

> I am very pleased with our execution as a company. We delivered on our commitments to you, our shareholders, to our partners, and to our customers. We changed where we needed to, built around our core products, our channel and services strength, while prioritizing our resources to our five foundational areas. Each of us as a Cisco employee takes pride in our earning per share growth twice as fast as revenue in FY 2012.

Cisco, by the nature of both the company's founding principles and the nature of their work, already had a leg up compared to other companies in that it had already successfully leveraged social tools for engagement in the workplace. What makes this case especially interesting is the company's realization that social integration in itself wasn't enough. In the face of important decisions, the company realized it needed buy-in from its employees at a very fundamental level, and quickly worked to leverage its tools to facilitate an open arena for engagement. The company may not have had all the answers to comprehensively implement this process right away, but its leaders were unafraid to jump in and develop effective best practices for engagement and measurement as they needed them.

CHAPTER 9

How the Southwest Way Creates Competitive Advantage

When we asked Dana Williams, Director of Integrated Marketing and Communications at Southwest Airlines, whether her company was a social brand, we could almost hear her shrug her shoulders on the other end of the line. "We've always been a social brand," she said matter-of-factly. "We just evolved and have more channels to do it now." This confidence, this absolute certainty of brand mission, is apparent in everything the company does. Because of this, it should come as no surprise that Southwest Airlines has helped lead the social employee charge into the twenty-first century.

The company's earliest incarnation came in 1967, when Air Southwest Co. was incorporated under founders Rollin King and Herb Kelleher. From the beginning, King and Kelleher infused the company with a single driving philosophy: the business of businesses was people. To keep those people coming back, the company had a responsibility to take care of its employees. Happy employees treat customers with the dignity they deserve. Even with this dogged sense of brand identity, Southwest has faced challenges in building a unified corporate culture that is largely unique to the airline industry. The following success story examines the methods Southwest Airlines has employed to keep the concept of social business fresh, the challenges of communicating with a multigenerational employee base

Figure 9.1

Southwest Airlines founder Herb Kelleher posing on the wing of a plane.
Credit: Southwest Airlines

spread across the continent, and the techniques the brand employs to ensure customer satisfaction through a thriving employee culture (see Figure 9.1).

Born Conversationalists

It's the opinion of the executives at Southwest that the brand has always been in contact with its customers, despite the fact that it has had the benefit of measurable insights through data collection only for the past four or five years. Even before the advent of digital media and social technology, Southwest insisted on being attentive to customer needs by quickly and enthusiastically responding to each letter and phone call. As Dana Williams put it, "We knew what our customers wanted because they were always talking to us and we were always talking to them."

In this way, the brand's mission has always been one of social/customer engagement. When we spoke with Christi McNeill, the Senior Social and Emerging Media Specialist at Southwest, she likened the interactivity provided by social media as a better version of the "letters to the editor" model. Through social technology, customers are afforded the opportunity to talk about the good, the bad, and the ugly regarding their experience with a brand, and they expect their voices to be heard.

Southwest is the largest airline in the United States in terms of passengers, carrying over 100 million travelers across the country each year. Coordinating the travel plans of these millions of customers, not to mention its large network of employees—pilots, flight attendants, airport workers, and more—takes a special kind of proactivity and finesse, especially in an era when "Airports have dynamically changed since 9/11," as Dana Williams stated. With a large amount of its workforce working remotely, Southwest sees employees as an essential lifeline to its customers.

Founder Herb Kelleher once famously said, "If the employee comes first, then they're happy. . . . A motivated employee treats the customer well. The customer is happy so they keep coming back, which pleases the shareholders. It's not one of the enduring green mysteries of all time; it is just the way it works." Dana Williams echoes this sentiment. "Every decision we make is focused on employees first. Our employees are the essence of our brand." To achieve this, Southwest honed its employee-first culture over the years, working tirelessly to be transparent in keeping crews in all corners of the continent apprised of everything going on within the brand.

Early Social Business: The Culture Committee

Longtime Southwest employee Colleen Barrett began working for the company as cofounder Herb Kelleher's secretary, but quickly rose through the organizational ranks to become executive vice president in the 1990s and president of the company from 2001 to 2008. During the 1990s, Barrett began hosting quarterly meetings with hand-selected employees from various parts of the company. She brought various workers together, such as mechanics, pilots, flight attendants, and accountants, to talk about what was going on in the company. As Dana Williams said, "When you're in the airline business, not everybody's at the same office every day, so culture is important to manage and protect." Barrett's solution to this concern was simple: meet with the employees, give them a voice, and learn about that culture firsthand (see Figure 9.2).

Figure 9.2

The Culture Committee: Former Southwest President Colleen Barrett poses with a group of employees.

Credit: Southwest Airlines

Barrett's meetings quickly came to be known as the Culture Committee. Through them, Barrett was able to keep her finger on the pulse of the brand, building a broad knowledge base of what her employees needed and how the leaders could help to facilitate those needs. The Culture Committee, which is still very much in practice today, takes charge of various employee outreach activities to grease the wheels of productivity, ensuring that day-to-day activities run smoothly and enjoyably. Throughout the years, the Committee has been in charge of such tasks as cleaning the planes between flights (what the employees affectionately refer to as the "Hokey Days") or setting up food stations for maintenance and crew bases late at night or early in the morning.

When employees are on the Culture Committee, they're not just learning about what's happening within the brand from some distant boardroom. The Culture Committee is out into the field to take part in daily activities and learn about what's happening at the employee and customer level so more useful suggestions can be taken back to the group.

In late 2010, when Southwest acquired AirTran Airways, the Culture Committee created a mission to ensure that all employee groups were in sync and helping each other acclimate to the new working environment. Because of this proactive initiative—as well as the strength of AirTran's own employee culture—the transition went off without a hitch. The Culture Committee helped acclimate AirTran employees to the Southwest way of doing things, showing them that it was okay to have fun, loosen their ties, sing a song, or tell a joke from time to time.

Reframing for Two-Way Communication

While Southwest made every effort to keep employees informed through transparent, earnest communication, it didn't have the infrastructure in place to offer an automated way to generate employee feedback. In the spring of 2006, Southwest began a biennial survey of its employees in an effort to learn as much as possible about what was thought about the goings-on within the brand. In the first survey, Southwest was overwhelmed when it found that most employees craved a better platform for offering feedback. The company began to envision a two-way communication process where ideas and news could be exchanged more efficiently, and everybody would be given the opportunity to be heard.

Southwest had implemented the SWALife intranet system in 2004 to offer employees real-time news for workers out on the front lines. It wasn't until the SWALife Interactive upgrade in 2010 that employees were able to contribute to the conversation as well. This internal intranet platform is capable of delivering information specific to both departments and individuals. Employees now had easy, secure access to paycheck or talent review information from any location.

Within the SWALife Interactive platform, there is an employee blog. This blog posts three to six internal stories every day—with subjects ranging from important company initiatives and messages from its CEO and other leaders to employee volunteer activities and company history. Southwest also communicates quarterly earnings results, and has developed a dashboard to track progress on company goals. When certain goals are met, employees are rewarded. Employees can leave comments on any blog post, and all comments are closely moderated by members of the Communication Team. All comments are tied to a specific employee's account—no anonymous commenting is allowed. In order to participate, employees must first agree to a set of Terms and Conditions that dictate blog behavior. Every employee profile on SWALife contains basic information such as name, location, and position. Profiles are also highly customizable, allowing workers to add a profile photo and other personal information not related to work.

"Our philosophy with the blog is that employees are having these conversations out in the field already—at least this way we can participate, and keep a pulse on the general employee sentiment," said Todd Painter, Communication Manager who oversees the employee blog. "The feedback our employees provide is invaluable to the company, because it shapes future messages, identifies issues needing attention that might otherwise have gone unnoticed, and provides a space for employee conversation. It helps connect employees from across our system."

Social Media Policy

To ensure that external engagement is transparent, Southwest posts a copy of its social media policy online. While internal guidelines go into far more depth than the elements listed here, these are the primary tenets the brand follows[1]:

1. **Follow Southwest standards (the Golden Rule):** Employees are responsible for their actions on the Internet and are encouraged not to post materials that may reflect negatively on Southwest.
2. **Employee identification:** Employees engaging in conversations about the brand should disclose that they are Southwest employees—although they aren't speaking on behalf of Southwest Airlines. Employee profiles should include a similar disclaimer.
3. **Be an ambassador:** Employees should strive to represent Southwest Airlines in the best way at all times.
4. **Shhh — it's a secret!:** Employees must keep confidential information confidential. If employees aren't sure whether information is public, they should not make it public.
5. **Respect the privacy of others:** Employees should assume that everything they post online will stay there forever, for anyone to see. Because of this, they should exercise discretion when discussing personal details—either their own or those of coworkers.
6. **Company trademarks and logos:** Employees may not use Southwest's logos, trademarks, and copyrighted materials without the express written permission of the Southwest Airlines Licensing Department in Marketing.
7. **Follow the rules:** Employees will not engage in illegal or unlawful activities, a policy that extends to posting copyrighted materials.
8. **Be accountable:** Employees are encouraged to report inappropriate behavior by Southwest employees.

Taking Social Participation Public

Interactivity does not end within the brand. Southwest is proud of employees using platforms like Facebook and Twitter. In fact, the company encourages this activity to whatever extent the employees are comfortable with—provided, of course, they follow the Southwest Airlines Social Media Policy. The brand views this kind of activity as a better way to help get its message out.

Another benefit of employee messaging is the ability to dramatically increase exposure for certain messages. For instance, whenever Southwest is promoting a big fare sale, it sees significant results through viral dissemination—including posting content though the SWALife platform and encouraging employees to share that content within their own networks. The brand will even help social employees with suggested messages and photos they can use.

Southwest's guiding rules for this kind of communication are defined and continually reinforced. We spoke with several ambassadors for the brand, and the word "encourage" constantly came up. Strong modeling of social media best practices among leadership becomes essential with this principle. Southwest doesn't mandate any employee to actively promote the brand, but by constantly modeling the process to demonstrate the benefits of social communication, management has found that employees are more than happy to participate.

Lessons in Social Outreach

To help paint a clearer picture of how Southwest socially engages customers through a variety of different circumstances, we asked Christi McNeill to provide a few examples of successful social interventions.

Kevin Smith—"Too Fat to Fly"

Around mid-February 2010, famed indie director Kevin Smith boarded a Southwest flight only to be told by Southwest employees that his physical condition posed a safety and seating concern for the rest of the passengers on the flight. Therefore, the flight staff said, he would not be able to travel. Incensed, the director took to Twitter and began deriding the company for deciding he was "too fat to fly." Twitter had a well-established presence in the social sphere in 2010, and this incidence proved a unique challenge to the social media team at Southwest. How did they respond to the director's concerns authentically and with integrity without the event turning into a PR nightmare?

As the story began to take on a life of its own on Twitter and various news sites, Southwest leapt into action on multiple fronts. First, representatives reached out publicly to Smith via Twitter, apologizing for the incidence and offering assistance. Second, other representatives got Smith on the phone to engage with him directly and ensure that communication channels remained open. Third, Smith was booked on the next available flight free of charge, and given a rebate for his missed flight. The incident may have begun with a mistake, but Southwest was determined to turn it into a victory.

The entire event may not have cast the brand in the most favorable light at first, but it also offered an incredible opportunity for the brand to put policy into practice by publicly repairing its relationship with Smith. Southwest representatives ensured that their response was as transparent and open as possible. Through employee ambassadors, the brand not only admitted fault for incorrectly removing Smith from the flight, it even posted about the experience on the Southwest blog. As McNeill wrote in her post:

> It is not our customary method of Customer Relations to be so public in how we work through these situations, but with so many people involved in the occurrence, you also should be involved in the solution. First and foremost, to Mr. Smith; we would like to echo our Tweets and again offer our heartfelt apologies to you. We are sincerely sorry for your travel experience on Southwest Airlines.[2]

While no brand wants to be involved on the negative end of a story like this, Southwest used the incidence to learn about its own policies and reconsider how it engages both socially and in the work-place. As McNeill related to us in our conversation about the event:

> The experience actually led us to really evaluate how our social media team works together. We were able to come out of this situation with a better understanding of how we could equip ourselves behind the scenes to handle issues such as this.

Damaged Baggage

Another opportunity for brand ambassadorship came in the form of a damaged suitcase. Over the holidays one year, the Southwest Social Media Team discovered a website (http://dearswa.com/), which had apparently been created by a disappointed customer in order to air his grievances regarding a recent experience with the airline.

The customer's letter presents his experience through a series of witty pop culture puns and images, referencing movies such as *Home Alone*, *A Christmas Story*, and *The Nightmare Before Christmas*. The customer began the account by explaining first and foremost that he was a "big fan" of the brand. However, he had just purchased a new suitcase for his Christmas vacation only to find that it had been significantly damaged during transport. Further, the customer explained that the Southwest representative at the baggage claim hadn't been helpful, which prompted him to reach out by posting a web page.

The message may have been public, but it was also conciliatory, clearly offering Southwest the opportunity to make amends. The Social Media Team was happy to oblige, and responded with an apology letter crafted in a similar fashion as the original message (http://www.dearswa.com/swa-response.html). By doing so, the brand showed its human side by engaging the disappointed customer both publicly and in a way that demonstrated its own sense of humor. Aside from offering an apology, Southwest also gave the customer a refund on the flight and a check for a new suitcase. The customer, clearly pleased with the response, even posted Southwest's follow-up letter to his website as a companion piece to the original. As a result of the encounter, Southwest gained a valuable brand advocate, whose website has essentially become a testimonial for the brand's social outreach efforts.

Credit: http://www.dearswa.com/swa-response.html

"The Most Remarkably Kind Flight Attendant"

Not all social media encounters have to begin with a grievance, of course. Sometimes social outreach can end up being just good, plain fun. As detailed on the Southwest blog,[3] the story began when a Southwest flight attendant named Holly had a chance encounter with a passenger who turned out to be none other than the father of country superstar Taylor Swift. The man was so impressed with Holly's efforts that he gave her a few of Taylor's guitar picks that he happened to have on hand.

On the very next flight, Holly met a couple who turned out to be big Taylor Swift fans. So, remembering her encounter with Swift's father from earlier in the day, Holly generously offered up a few of Swift's guitar picks to the passengers. These travelers were thrilled, and immediately used the in-flight Wi-Fi to post a message to Southwest's Social Media Team:

If someone in the Southwest Airlines corporate HQ can see this— I'm on flight 913 currently en route to Phoenix and I want y'all to know that our flight attendant Holly is perhaps one of the most remarkably kind and helpful people my girlfriend and I have ever met. If you can meet us at the gate with something remarkable for this remarkable woman (a promotion, a raise, a Chipotle burrito, anything), I will sign a document pledging to only fly Southwest from here on out (unless you do not fly where I need to go). Of course—I request a "Keyman Clause" in this agreement stipulating the contract terminates if Holly ever leaves. People like her are why I fly SWA.

The Southwest team in Phoenix received the message immediately, and began coordinating a surprise for the unassuming flight attendant. Once the flight landed, Holly was presented with a giant chocolate chip cookie that said "Holly, most remarkably kind flight attendant" on top, as well as a corresponding sash. Further, the passenger made good on his promise, and signed an impromptu contract saying he would indeed only fly Southwest exclusively as long as Holly remained employed with the company.

Encounters such as these breathe life into a brand and drive customer experiences to the next level. The Southwest team could just as easily have read the customer's message and simply passed it along to Holly as positive feedback. Instead, Southwest chose to take engagement to the next level, simultaneously demonstrating its commitment to both its employees and its customers.

Training

Southwest builds its social employees' knowledge base on a quarterly basis, continually moving forward with new trainings, policies, and additional support. Social connectivity tools assist the brand tremendously in these quarterly webinars, helping the company to efficiently communicate with employees who are spread all across the nation. In these webinars, employees call in to learn about current campaigns, new ways the brand is employing social media, and new updates on social media policy. During this process, the brand also hopes that employees take the information gained through the webinars and share it with their coworkers.

According to Todd Painter, Communication Manager at Southwest:

We encourage our employees to be the voice behind certain messages. Whether it's on our external or internal blog, a majority of our blog posts come from our employees. It's not necessarily somebody at our headquarters—we reach out and encourage employees from varying locations, departments, and positions to get their name out there and to own subjects as appropriate. I think that adds authenticity to our channels and messages when our employees get to hear from their peers.

How Have the Employees Responded to Their Roles?

As far as activating employees and getting them to participate in the digital village, every Southwest ambassador we spoke with agreed that motivation hasn't been a problem. Because being social and sharing a sense of connectivity was so ingrained in the company's culture long before the advent of social media, these tools merely served as extensions of the brand's culture. "Our employees are our biggest fans," Todd Painter said. Because of this, Southwest employees generally have very little problem being willing to adapt to the new digital environment.

Inevitably, social engagement just isn't a good fit for some employees. Because Southwest doesn't have a mandatory buy-in policy to these social media programs, such instances pose little problem for either the brand or the employee. Further, some employees simply don't have time to engage in social media. As Painter explained, the brand naturally seeks out the employees who are engaged and passionate about social media whether at work or at home. The latter type of brand ambassador is more than willing to help spread Southwest's message through digital channels, so it becomes a win-win for all parties involved.

Minding the Generation Gap

Christi McNeill pointed out the Southwest community houses four generations of employees. This fact, coupled with the reality that a significant portion of the airline's employees are "absentee" (always traveling), means that Southwest has had to learn how to deliver its message simultaneously via multiple channels. By doing so, the brand has ensured that every employee, regardless of age or physical location, has the opportunity to learn and contribute. Southwest provides communication through:

▶ a monthly magazine
▶ a phone line that provides weekly updates from Southwest executives
▶ SWALife, as well as a fully interactive mobile version of the SWALife app
▶ Company email (all SWALife content can also be accessed via email, and every employee has a Southwest email account)
▶ Text messages for breaking company headlines (employees must opt in to receive)
▶ Daily, one-page printed newsletters (with the same content as is communicated in the company email and on SWALife) posted to common bulletin boards placed in high employee traffic locations throughout the system.

In this way, social media facilitates the communication process, but the concept of social business practice is extended beyond simple software tools. Said McNeill, "The most important part of our communication strategy is that we don't just focus on social media. It's a huge piece of how we communicate, but there are so many other ways that we reach out."

Crisis Management

Southwest is a major airline and is often on the frontlines of crisis management, coordinating complex activities with mobile personnel across great distances. Aside from keeping employees informed, safe, and ready for action, the brand also has a responsibility to maintain transparency with customers and to offer assistance where needed.

The events of September 11, 2001, offered a compelling glimpse into the brand's dedication to communication and assistance, despite the fact the occurrence happened years before most businesses had adopted social networking platforms. According to Dana Williams, feedback from both customers and employees indicated that the brand worked tirelessly to maintain open communication channels during the aftermath of the terrorist attacks. At the time, the only efficient way to spread information was often through phone calls. Speaking on the brand's efforts, Williams said, "This goes back to managing the brand from the inside out. We've got to take care of our employees first so they can take care of their customers and tell them what's going on."

During that time, many Southwest planes had to land in airports that the airline didn't service, which meant that pilots and flight attendants had no access to ground support or resources once they'd landed. Naturally, the many passengers on the planes were in a state of disarray as well. However, Williams mentioned several instances of the flight staff stepping up to the plate during those moments to offer whatever support they could.

In one instance, Williams recalled a Southwest pilot personally assisting all passengers off the plane and ordering them pizza with his credit card. Another pilot took similar steps by buying the passengers Amtrak tickets to help them get to their destinations after all planes had been grounded. As Williams said:

> We have a legacy with our customers who have been with us a long time, who know that we're going to get them there on time. We're going to get them where they need to go, and, if we can't, we're going to tell them about it and we're going to help with whatever we can do to make it happen, no matter what problems come our way. Our business is about making stories for people and helping them through their lives with their own stories. Not only the employees, but the customers.

Such dedication and forward thinking on the behalf of Southwest employees shows that certain needs do not change in the age of social media. The truth is that employee culture has always been important, and brands like Southwest that have always prized this trait have had a much easier time transitioning to social business models.

Applying Crisis Lessons to Hurricane Sandy

Within a week of our initial interviews with the employee representatives at Southwest, Hurricane Sandy struck the east coast, devastating our home state of New Jersey along with the rest of the New England coastline. As we sat powerless in our home, safe from most of the devastation brought on by the storm, we found ourselves wondering how Southwest's crisis management team was responding to this disaster, and how social media had helped to further improve the brand's responsiveness since 9/11 (see Figure 9.3).

During the hurricane, Southwest employees took a "better safe than sorry" approach to everything. During weather events such as Sandy, the company deploys what it calls the Weather Disruption

Figure 9.3

New Orleans Fire Department Captain Steve Lambert prepares to board a Southwest flight on his way to assist with Hurricane Sandy relief.

Credit: Southwest Airlines

Task Force. This group gathers in a designated disaster room to closely monitor significant weather events until the threat has passed. SWALife and Southwest.com played central roles in coordinating activities and keeping both employees and customers up to date on things such as cancellations and rerouted flights. The site offered regular updates on the operational impact of the hurricane, and also pointed employees and customers to further resources about cancellations and other changes.[4] Publicly, Southwest provided regular updates via southwest.com in coordination with Southwest's social channels, updating customers regarding affected airports and flights.

Southwest also reached out to the communities impacted by the storm and offered to help with disaster relief. New Orleans firefighters, eager to repay the State of New York for the assistance their own firefighters offered in the aftermath of Hurricane Katrina, hitched free rides on Southwest planes.[5] Southwest also offered its services for animal rescue efforts. Crew members donated their time and resources to transport 60 orphaned dogs, cats, and other animals from Long Island.[6] This kind of dedication and generosity among Southwest employees comes naturally as a result of the corporate culture, which is only magnified in times of crisis.

One other story often lost in disaster situations like Hurricane Sandy is the loss of employee homes, the company, or both. During Hurricane Sandy, although no employees were killed or injured as a result of the storm, several employees' homes were either lost or damaged. Leaders at Southwest quickly sprang into action, offering support groups and other resources for their employees to help transition through a challenging period.

Key Takeaways

Culture Drives Social Policy

When asked what is required of Southwest to make sure its brand stands out from the competition in the minds of both its employees and its customers, Dana Williams replied, "It sounds so complicated, but it's so darn easy sometimes. It's just doing the right thing."

To illustrate this, Williams pointed to one of their more recent ad campaigns, where Southwest used the line, "The Airline that changed the game for the entire industry." Southwest's laser-like focus on customer service has emerged in many business decisions, such as the "Bags fly free" policy and the Rapid Rewards program, which offers practical perks (e.g., no expiration, no blackout dates) to its customers that many other airlines do not.

Measuring Communication Success

In addition to the biennial employee surveys we mentioned earlier, Southwest also monitors success through regular communication channel audits. This involves the brand's Communication team reaching out to a random set of employees to get perspectives on how valuable or effective certain communication tools are. One benefit that has arisen from the integration of social platforms into the brand's operational structure is that the brand is better able to collect and measure employee satisfaction with new initiatives.

Todd Painter pointed out that the process is constantly evolving, just as the social media world is. When weighing employee feedback against new developments in the tech world, the brand's primary focus is on whether a certain change fits Southwest's culture and business needs. The brand views the transition to social media strategies as a means of improving existent structures and mindsets, and not as reinventing the wheel.

Recently, the brand has been developing social media education programs for its executives (for more on social executives, see Chapter 12). In many of our other success stories, we have stressed the importance of social employee practices being driven from the C-Suite down. In this case, Southwest Airlines is a somewhat anachronistic example. The brand's executives do remain highly engaged in employee activities such as the Culture Committee, the weekly phone updates, and the conversation on SWALife, and in those ways they are highly effective in driving social practices. Because the brand has maintained its focus on culture over tools, their approach isn't altogether that surprising, and is once again demonstrative of our maxim: every brand has to find its own way in the digital bazaar. As Dana Williams said, "We try to do things the Southwest Way instead of the legacy way."

CHAPTER 10

AT&T: B2B Social Networking at Its Best

A T&T can trace its roots all the way back to the advent of telecommunication and Alexander Graham Bell. Over a nearly 140-year history, AT&T has persevered through a wide variety of changes—both internally and externally driven—and emerged triumphant throughout all of it.

Redefining Leadership

Today, AT&T is a leading provider of IP networking and wireless services in the United States, and brings a diverse array of adjacent technology services and solutions to business customers. The AT&T digital marketing team researched the patterns of B2B customers, from the smallest local business to the most complex global enterprise. The team found that patterns were rapidly changing, so they began to diversify their approach to customer engagement. New ways to embrace digital channels and use social media were needed. Something had to be created that would enable customers and potential clients to gain access to the expertise of their in-house technology specialists and industry thought leaders.

The AT&T Networking Exchange Blog

In order to expand its effective reach and to influence B2B technology purchase decisions, AT&T created the Networking Exchange Blog. The digital marketing team understood that producing engaging, authentic blog content meant that it needed to place a premium on the value of the content, and the role of person-to-person influence. The goals were to (1) provide helpful content for customers on diverse IT and business topics, and (2) expand trust and influence by empowering its employees to become more visible brand ambassadors. As stated on the AT&T blog homepage, the intended value of the Networking Exchange Blog is for clients to "Connect, engage and innovate with our network and technology experts, and explore new ways to power your business." The posts on the blog are largely focused on enabling readers to understand technology trends, discover best practices and spark ideas for business model innovation. Product and solution selling takes a strong backseat to the power of bigger ideas and discovery of technology insights. This capitalizes on a "truth" in the B2B social sphere in particular: enterprises are selling to *people* who happen to make decisions for business entities. The seamless integration of these efforts creates the truly social brand—combining expertise, culture, process, relationships, and trust.

By looking first within its own walls for its thought leaders, AT&T quickly built a vibrant community of employee bloggers who were more than happy to provide their perspective on issues and trends within the industry. To supplement this process, AT&T also launched what it called the Networking Leaders Academy. This blogging community of practice was designed to provide support, education, encouragement, and guidelines for employees as they ventured out into the digital bazaar.

Through a constant stream of new content produced by a group of social-savvy employees adept at leveraging their own social networks in order to promote content, traffic to the Networking Exchange Blog rose quickly. AT&T had achieved its initial goals faster than expected, and soon thereafter, new ways to expand its efforts were sought.

Building Community Externally

After Networking Exchange Blog steadily increased its authority as a B2B technology resource, AT&T decided to expand the program to include outside experts offering additional topic diversity. In late 2011, Blue Focus Marketing became a contributing voice to help guide best practices in small business branding and marketing. Later, other external contributors were added to deepen coverage of SMB marketing and technology topics.

By enriching blog content to include contributions from outside experts, both AT&T and the outside writers would benefit from the increased exposure. One of Blue Focus Marketing's initial goals was to help small businesses understand the value of social media marketing. In our experiences, we have heard many representatives at companies say things like, "Let's do social media" without thinking about why they were doing it and what benefit their customers might get out of it. One of our initial focuses as a social business, then, was to show how social media could help businesses humanize their brands. A fundamental trait of the social age is the fact that people expect information to come from a trusted resource with a human face. Through the AT&T Networking Exchange Blog, the digital marketing team understood this essential element of what it meant to be a social brand, so the project seemed like a good fit for both parties.

As the first of only a handful of external bloggers, we posted on social media topics such as employee branding, social branding, content marketing, social business, and social media in crisis management. This arrangement between independent bloggers and AT&T proved quickly to be successful.

The experience of working with AT&T planted a seed in our minds that would eventually grow into the content of this book, as illustrated in the Blue Focus Marketing post "The Rise of the Employee Brand."[1]

Increasing Engagement

The innovative approach used by AT&T created an authentic B2B content model to engage small businesses, and could very well serve as a role model for other brands as they form their own blogging communities.

The blog's success hasn't caused AT&T to rest on its laurels, however. In late 2012, the blog underwent a redesign to further boost reader engagement. The new design prizes content and accessibility, offering a clean, modern format that utilizes recent best practices for content marketing—such as infographics, best-of lists, striking visual navigation, ease of use, and open-ended questions for readers. The re-envisioned site also allows users to engage with the site in new ways, including enhanced email subscription and following an individual contributor via RSS.

With AT&T's ongoing commitment to creating engaging content through its network of employees and external bloggers, the brand is poised to remain a vital resource for cutting-edge marketing practices as small businesses continue to learn what social means to them.

CHAPTER 11

How Acxiom and Domo Are Leading the Charge

We came across a wealth of inspiring stories while working to better illuminate the social employee journey at brands across the globe. The brands in this chapter are making great strides in their social employee initiatives, and deserve recognition for their efforts. Whether it's the PACT at Acxiom or the #domosocial program at Domo, these brands help to further illustrate a crucial point in the social branding process. Chiefly, brands must find their own way so it can be discovered what works best. While we have learned that most of the brands we spoke to applied the same general philosophies and guiding rules while making the transition to social, the specific details governing them tend to be quite different. This chapter examines some of the more innovative social initiatives we uncovered and the methods used to generate thriving social programs.

Acxiom: The Social Employee PACT

Acxiom is a data, analytics, and software company that works to strengthen connections between people, businesses, and their partners. In order to achieve this, the company must connect and analyze data, help organizations better know their customers, personalize customer experiences, and assist in creating higher levels of engagement.

Acxiom specializes in connecting partners and creating software that promotes optimization of customer value.

With over 6,600 associates working to serve more than 7,000 brands around the world, Acxiom has learned a great deal about the benefits of social business practices when coordinating operations. According to Tim Suther, Chief Marketing and Strategy Officer at Acxiom, the brand must securely provide close to a trillion different customer updates for its clients each week. This involves making coordinated, decentralized communication an absolute necessity if the brand seeks to avoid unwanted silos. To address this need, the brand has empowered every Acxiom associate to participate in social media, guided by a universal set of engagement principles.

Consumer-Driven Culture

As Suther observes, "Modern brands live in the era of empowered consumers, who have unlimited choice and information about those choices. They choose when, where, how, and *whether* they engage with brands." For the marketing technologists at Acxiom, it has become vital for the brand to glean insights from all relevant data, and to apply that information wherever it matters. One strategy the brand has employed is a policy of being flexible and nimble. This means being ready to adapt best practices and engagement methods as needed without encountering any friction in the process.

Suther had an interesting analogy for Acxiom's social adoption process: "Like the difference between reading about riding a bike and actually riding it, the key in social is to be actually in it—participating, monitoring, being part of the conversation, and thoughtfully building networks." As part of Acxiom's core DNA, the brand expects to strengthen its bonds between people, businesses, and their partners by providing progressive communication while focusing on being innovative (creating cutting-edge products and services), analytical (data-driven smarts), trustworthy (a neutral and secure connector of partners), and authentic (genuine and experienced). To achieve this, Acxiom operates by a set of principles it calls PACT:

▶ **Passion:** Encapsulated by the statement "This company is my company," associates are asked to believe in and support the mission, act with purpose, care about one another, and bring energy to everything they do.

▸ **Accountability:** Summed up in the statement "Do the right thing. Own the outcome." Associates are asked to make a difference, take the initiative, embrace the challenge, solve the problem, and deliver results.

▸ **Creativity:** The overarching idea is to "Unleash the possibilities" whereby associates need to think outside the norm, imagine what could be, dare to take intelligent risks, learn from experience and share it, and innovate on behalf of clients.

▸ **Teamwork:** The essence is "Winning together," and associates do so by collaborating and challenging one another, trusting and being trustworthy, leveraging strength and differences, building relationships, celebrating successes, and having fun along the way.

Training

PACT provides a solid foundation for social engagement, but the brand also regularly updates a more in-depth online guide to social media. Acxiom's annual privacy and security training also provides additional guidance on the appropriate use of information on social networks. The annual training requires that each associate complete a certification in privacy and compliance.

Building on that foundation, in 2011 the brand also released Marketing IQ, a package designed with the goal of making marketing and media simple. Marketing IQ offers a library of over 30 videos, access to "brain food," a jargon decoder, and a list of the top books and thought leaders in social media. These resources help create Acxiom associates who are well equipped to discuss the latest in marketing and media in both social and conventional channels.

Coordinating On the Go

The digital revolution has lifted the anchors of the workplace, allowing employees to sail the seven seas of commerce with greater ease than ever before. As we discussed in Chapter 4, the social employee expects to be able to work both remotely and on the go. In order to help facilitate that process, Acxiom introduced an app in 2012. The app enables associates to receive updates regarding all aspects of the Acxiom DNA—including articles, blog posts, and video clips from leaders across the organization. The brand is very proud of the mobile solution and has seen employee engagement go up considerably as a result.

Employee Response

We had the chance to connect with a couple Acxiom associates to learn more about their experiences as social employees:

Mark Donatelli, Experienced Global Marketing and Technology Leader

I think that my involvement in social media has helped human- ize the brand by the fact that I am a working professional, living Acxiom's business day in and day out, and I take the time to share relevant content and commentary. My network of con- nections views the information as coming from someone in the trenches like them, as opposed to someone in marketing churn- ing out 140-character snippets.

I do feel more connected with customers—simple things like a headshot, stream of tweets, and a LinkedIn profile go a long way in providing a way to get to know each other as your busi- ness relationship develops. You can tell who "works" somewhere and who is passionate about what they do—that goes both ways. And as you know, the connections live on beyond the company's relationship as well. I would like to spend more time on this type of work, but frankly it is hard to do sometimes with the demands of my "day job."

Allison Nicholas, College Recruiting/University Relations

My goal is always to share meaningful information that is inter- esting, timely, and helpful. I appreciate the opportunity to use social media tools as part of my job. Social media for me also

serves as a dynamic learning environment where I can play the
role of a student, tutor, or teacher. The immediate access to so
many great minds and resources is very rewarding. Thanks to
social media, my family and friends better understand my job
and my crazy schedule.

Social Recruiting

Aside from sharing her feelings on what it's like to work for a social brand like Acxiom, Allison Nicholas also provided us with an interesting anecdote on the power of social when it comes to recruiting student interns and employees. Nicholas reports that platforms such as Facebook dramatically increase Acxiom's visibility when it comes to placing people in jobs and internships. Before the interview and offer process involving one recent Acxiom hire, Nicholas says the prospective employee was actively engaged with the brand through Facebook, helping to keep conversations moving forward by answering questions and responding to comments.

These types of encounters often spill into the real world as well. Nicholas recounted another instance at a Walmart where she ran into a different student she had actively engaged on Facebook. According to Nicholas, the student immediately mentioned some job postings she had recently put up on their page. After expressing interest in those posts, the student then asked when Acxiom would be posting summer internship opportunities, and promised to drop Nicholas a note before applying to any during the spring.

Changing Minds One Person at a Time

Mark Ogne, who is in charge of Corporate Social Strategy, shared another social success story that he felt typified Acxiom's efforts on platforms like Twitter. After Acxiom put out a press release regarding a recent deal with Sony Ericsson, one Twitter user responded somewhat negatively to the two brands' media partnership, citing what he perceived to be Acxiom's own less-than-stellar social engagement practices.

Ogne saw an opportunity for engagement by responding to the comment, and quickly reached out to the man. This particular Twitter user had established himself as influential in the industry through an active Twitter followership. The two exchanged messages back and forth, with Ogne asking for an opportunity to change the user's mind about Acxiom. Eventually, the conversation led to a chance for a person-to-person meeting in London. During that meeting, Ogne was able to paint a more detailed picture of Acxiom's social evolutionary process over the past few years.

The Twitter user emerged from the conversation impressed with both Acxiom as a social brand and Ogne for his stellar advocacy efforts. As a result, the user publicly recanted his previous stance on Acxiom. In fact, the encounter proved so effective that the Twitter user became an active supporter of the brand online, and even promised to write a feature on Acxiom for a future blog post. This example perfectly demonstrates the value brands such as Acxiom must now place on brand advocacy through authentic, individual social engagement on social platforms. Turnabouts as in this example don't just succeed in changing the mind of one user, they also ripple out through the user's own network, building stock in social capital along the way.

Results and Recognition

Since Acxiom first implemented the PACT program, the brand has seen tremendous results:

- ▶ Associate satisfaction is up in 20 of 20 categories measured by the brand.
- ▶ Associate engagement with internal communications is up 33 percent.
- ▶ Voluntary associate turnover is down 300 basis points.
- ▶ As of late 2012, Acxiom stock had risen 80 percent in the prior 12 months.

Aside from those encouraging statistics, many employees at the brand have also received recognition for their efforts. For instance, ExecRank named Warren Jensen, CFO, as one of the top CFOs in the

United States in 2012. In 2011, Jennifer Barnett-Glasgow, CPO, was the Privacy Vanguard Winner. Tim Suther, CMO, was listed as one of the "Top 2012 CMOs" by ExecRank, and earned #Nifty50 honors as part of a joint program with Blue Focus Marketing and Tom Pick's Webbiquity blog.

Full Speed Ahead

Suther echoed a common theme we heard among all our brands, namely, that executive leadership had to walk the walk with employees in order to see adoption rates go up.

Executive-level commitment and participation was vital in overcoming that challenge. Moreover, the Acxiom PACT was developed by a cross-functional team that represented every major discipline at Acxiom. As the leaders developed the plan, they felt they *owned* it. That was crucial for adoption.

Acxiom has been very happy with the engagement and enthusiasm on the part of its employees, but it has also acknowledged that the work of the social business is never done. "While pleased with our progress, we are not satisfied," Suther said. Social engagement through platforms like Chatter is still relatively new to the brand, and only recently expanded to become an enterprisewide connection solution. Nevertheless, the employees at Acxiom are excited for what the future might bring, and look forward to innovating new methods of client-employee engagement.

Domo: Going Social in Public

Domo is a software-as-a-service company that aims to give executives direct access to all the business data they need in one place with its innovative cloud-based software. The company markets to CEOs and other business users for whom access to relevant business data is often too complex, too expensive, and too slow. Domo first entered the scene in 2010, so it has a distinction among the brands we've worked with in that a majority of social media platforms and technologies actually predate the company. As the company declares on its website, "Domo transforms the way executives manage their businesses and drives value from the tens of billions of dollars that's been spent on traditional business intelligence systems." Domo is a business built for the digital village, with a stated purpose of helping to guide other brands into greener pastures.

The brand's youth and mission mean that Domo hasn't had to deal with navigating the transition into social that older businesses are experiencing. Instead, its mission has been one of pioneering, of putting policy to practice while simultaneously advising other brands to do the same. While such a process may be somewhat of a tightrope walk, the employees at Domo have already proven capable of rising to the challenge.

The #Domosocial Experiment

According to Domo Founder, CEO, and Chairman of the Board Josh James, "At Domo, we've made an effort to attract the right folks and certainly have pockets of bleeding-edge technologists and highly social Domosapiens."[1] To be competitive in an era where more technology start-ups sprout up daily, Domo employees have had to be industry leaders at understanding and leveraging social and technology trends. If not accomplished, they would risk being replaced by other brands that might do it better.

The #domosocial experiment began as "subterfuge," as James called it. Aside from the five employees—executive Julie Kehoe, a social media employee, a graphic designer, and two tech experts— at the 130-person start-up involved in designing the program, #domosocial was a complete surprise. Its purpose was twofold: (1) to produce 100 percent employee adoption of social media within the brand and (2) to produce a real-time public case study of the process. The program was announced in a blog post an hour before a company meeting. People following James on his blog or Twitter had a one hour advance notice of the program. Everyone else was completely in the dark until the program's launch.

Purpose and Design

As James said in his post, "For new employees, social savvy will be a prerequisite. For current employees, it will be a condition of employment. We are instituting a social IQ test into our hiring process. We mean business."[2] The idea of making the brand's social adoption process public arose from the nature of the new technologies and processes that were being adopted. In truth, all brands must adopt social media transparently and in real time, but Domo was perhaps the first brand to call attention to the very act of this process. Experimenting with new technology is an essential part of social business, and because of this, James was unafraid of any missteps Domo employees may take on their journey toward social literacy.

In fact, even the missteps would gain attention, and were a part of the program's design. Domo posted regular updates to the project page (www.domo.com/social), a hub designed to illustrate and critique the employee social adoption process, as well as provide tools and material to employees. During the eight-week stint, employees were expected to complete 29 different tasks. After the initial phase of the project was complete, new badges of accomplishment continued to be introduced every few months to ensure continued use of social tools on the part of employees.

Measuring Results

Domo performed a baseline quiz to measure the "Social IQ" of employees before the experiment began. At the conclusion of the eight-week period, the quiz was repeated. Results revealed a 19 percent increase in total score. Domo also found that, in terms of raw numbers, the experiment had been a success. As Julie Kehoe, Vice President of Communications, said:

> There were a couple of ways we quantified the impact of the experiment on our brand. The first was in the growth of our collective followers, which exposed our brand to a much bigger and more diverse audience than before the experiment.

Domo also found other positive indicators on social platforms (see Figure 11.1):

▶ Twitter followers increased by more than 300 percent.
▶ LinkedIn followers increased by 36 percent.
▶ Facebook followers increased by 28 percent.
▶ Pinterest followers increased by 91 percent.
▶ Tweets increased from an average of 80 to an average of 350 per day.
▶ Employees built over 200,000 connections and followers during the experiment.

Employees Are the Gateway to Brand Awareness

By the end of this experiment, there was a tremendous increase in brand exposure over a two-month period. According to Julie Kehoe, however, the most important outcome was not in the statistical bump in networking numbers, but in the Domo employees' response to the

Figure 11.1

How social can we get?

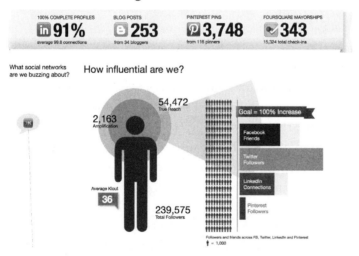

Credit: Domo

program. In addition to retaking the Social IQ quiz, Domo employees were asked how they felt about the program when everything was said and done.

Employees gave a variety of feedback, but the general consensus boiled down to two main factors: (1) they were very excited about the opportunity to learn new things, and (2) they enjoyed getting to know their fellow employees better and enjoyed a newfound sense of community within the organization. Further, before the experiment, 85.2 percent of employees agreed that social media belonged in business. After the experiment, 92.2 percent of employees agreed. The increase indicated the experiment's success in shifting perceptions about social media. As Kehoe said:

> *These answers were really the most meaningful to us. It showed that despite the time the experiment took, and getting some people to operate outside of their comfort zones, employees were truly excited to be a part of this.*

As a result of the #domosocial experiment, Kehoe reported that social has indeed become an integral part of company culture. Through its new culture of transparency, Domo executives have been able to learn more about the organization and the relationships within it that would otherwise have been completely off the radar. According to Kehoe, "You find pools of talent and natural alignment that you never would have discovered if you had maintained a traditional communications structure."

Benefits for Small Business

The executives at Domo found that social business practices help them stay close to customers, prospects, and employees, and also assist in responding to specific needs much more efficiently. Domo also found that the buzz surrounding its social policies helped attract new recruits. The brand developed a reputation for cutting-edge business practices, which is an attractive attribute to the incoming millennial generation of social employees (see Chapter 4). The flattened organizational structure also allowed Domo to increase efficiency by easily communicating and addressing company priorities among staff members.

The outside world has also taken notice. Domo has advised several Silicon Valley-based brands while considering similar organizational moves. Some employees from other organizations have actually followed Domo and its social certification process—live tweeting about the experience as they earned their social badges. Kehoe even noted with a touch of pride that a master's student out of New York had contacted the brand for inclusion in her thesis.

In all, the #domosocial program serves as a sterling example of the value to brands of jumping right into the fray. By taking a public, all-in approach, Domo incorporated liabilities that arose from the process as a part of the brand's story. The fearless leadership of CEO Josh James resulted in Domo becoming a paragon of cutting-edge social business practice, and a true social brand of the future.

PART III

Recalculating Your Route

CHAPTER 12

How Social Executives Drive Brand Value

Visibility is in the very DNA of what it means to be a social employee. It forms the foundation of every social business interaction, whether internally or externally. It's an inescapable truth, but it's also easily overlooked. After all, being visible simply isn't the way most of us are used to operating.

In traditional business models, executives would play the most visible roles at their companies, putting a friendly face on their brands whenever the need arose. While the era of the social employee has somewhat diffused that responsibility—almost anyone can occupy the spotlight at any given moment—the need for strong social leadership from the C-Suite has never been more important. Today, social media has made executives doubly visible. Their actions on social media platforms become scrutinized by both the public and their own employees.

This makes many executives uneasy, which is why so many of them tend to just avoid the problem altogether. Avoidance is an issue because in the digital village, an executive's absence often speaks louder than anything else. The social media silence that resonates from the C-Suites of most companies is both deafening and unsustainable. If executives want to steer their brands into the future, they must be prepared to lead by example. This chapter is our rallying cry for a new brand of leader—the social executive.

Why the Social Executive?

In a 2012 CEO Study, IBM found only 16 percent of the more than 1,700 chief executive officers surveyed were using social business platforms to connect with customers. More importantly, the IBM survey noted that the number of social executives was expected to jump to 57 percent within five years. In other words, executives may have been slow to transition up to this point, but they see the writing on the wall, and they know a change is coming. Because of this, there is nothing to lose by developing a social presence now. As our friend Kent Huffman, author of *8 Mandates* and CMO at BearCom Wireless, told us:

> *Social executives who build influence within communities now will wield tremendous power and influence with employees and customers down the road. Their early championing of social media will allow them to emerge as thought leaders within the industry, helping to guide the inevitable second wave of social executives into greener pastures.*

Social executives have the ability to drive culture by embodying their brand's mission, vision, and values. These executives drive change by walking the walk, embracing their companies' social platforms and modeling best practices for success. The value of the social executive impacts the core of a successful business in the modern age. By acting as a transparent, human model of brand values, the social executive activates the imagination of their employees. Our friend Alex Romanovich, Managing Partner of Social2B, Inc. and advisor to the CMO Club, elaborated on how executives can wield influence:

> *What is clear is that the social executive sets the cultural tone of the organization. Because social business brings greater individual freedom into the mix, executives have a responsibility as the most visible members of their organization to get their employees, and peer executives, on the same page by uniting*

them under a common purpose. Social executives act as guiding lights and the compasses for the organization across multiple functions—from marketing to technology to operations.

As we illustrated in our social business Möbius strip, the social executive catalyzes employees by establishing the brand's cultural values in the workplace, spurring workers into new levels of engagement. Recent figures show that, although nearly nine out of ten CMOs (or executives with related responsibilities) understand that social media has a measurable value for businesses,[1] an astounding 76 percent have zero social presence on Twitter.[2]

However, it is becoming increasingly clear that soon basic social media competency will be a prerequisite for all executive-level jobs. Once again, we're faced with the reality that trust in a brand drives its value, and a visible executive can help directly drive that trust. According to a BRANDfog survey, 82 percent of respondents said they were more likely to trust a brand whose executives engaged in social media, and 77 percent of respondents were more likely to buy from those companies as a result.[3]

These numbers indicate a redefinition of the role of the executive within the social business. So why haven't we seen more executives begin to take their first steps into the digital bazaar? The answers result largely from the environments in which most of these executives find themselves: they don't have time, they don't know where to get started, they're afraid of legal blowback, or they don't know how adding their own voice to the conversation will help anything.[4]

These reasons may appear somewhat mundane on the surface; nevertheless, they comprise the essential day-to-day realities of most executives. The truth is that executives will always be at odds with social business unless they can step out from underneath these realities and begin to drive change within their businesses. Taken as a whole, the move toward creating a culture of social executives appears to be a little bit of a "chicken and the egg" kind of problem; executives see the value, but they don't know how it fits into their day-to-day lives.

Social Is Not "In Addition To"

Sandy Carter, Vice President, Social Business Evangelism and Sales at IBM and one of our 2012 #Nifty50 Top Technical Women on Twitter, called the problem the "in addition to" mentality. Executives tend to look at social as another task they need to cram into their busy schedules, rather than something to be incorporated into—and enhance—an executive's daily duties. This is the reason businesses looking to upgrade to social models must do so multilaterally in order to drive change on all fronts and prevent social silos from forming. Embedding social activities into the business process yields effective incorporation into an executive's routine. If senior executives can leverage social in a way that fits into their daily work habits without it becoming a disruption, these executives will eventually become social advocates themselves. Carter gave us the following example:

> We work with the CEO of a large hotel chain who is used to dictating his messages. His assistant types them up and they go on their merry way. When IBM wanted to help him write an external blog, the question became: how do you marry dictation with writing a blog? He did not want someone to ghostwrite for him, so IBM embedded social methods into the way he blogs. The executive now dictates onto his iPhone. He can talk about what he wants to blog, and the program actually types the words. He then reviews it, hits a button, and the message gets posted to his blog. He is now blogging in a work style that is comfortable for him.

Carter also noted that several IBM executives began incorporating social by creating video blogs—an intuitive process that requires a very small learning curve. One Australian IBM leader uses the video feature on his iPad to interview customers about their experiences. He then posts the videos to his company blog to provide real-world examples of what is being said about the company. Video blogging often makes for an effective tool for many social executives because it's already a very familiar medium. As Carter said, "Part of the benefit of getting senior members to adopt is having them be comfortable with the way they get engaged and really leverage the methodologies of social."

As explained in Chapter 3, nobody is expected to have all the answers to every social media question or scenario right way. Some things just can't be taught—they have to be experienced. And, of course, some experiences can't be predicted. Sandy Carter also shared the story of Robert Niblock, Lowe's Chairman and CEO. When Niblock first began blogging, he heard some rumblings out in the community that he had a ghostwriter. The reason for these suspicions? Niblock was quite an accomplished writer, but he was a bit formal for the blog format, which usually takes a more relaxed tone.

The bottom line is that every platform has its own rules for engagement and presentation, but it's nearly impossible for a person to know all the nuances of a platform without having participated. The adjustment to a more suitable blogging tone wasn't hard for Niblock once he better understood the expectations of his audience. It took a few tries to get it right, and then he quickly rose to be one of the top bloggers Lowe's had. The most important takeaway from this example is not that Niblock learned to adapt his style, but rather that he never would have known what the appropriate style was unless he'd decided to participate.

David Edelman of McKinsey also sees the value of social executives engaging directly with employees, clients, and colleagues:

[T]he most important benefit of senior executives stepping into the social media mix is to hear the unvarnished voices who want to connect with them. With a fresh finger on the pulse of the external and internal buzz—and a good process for managing the flow—a senior executive can be better equipped to stand behind tough decisions, set new priorities, and begin reshaping a company's culture.[5]

New Data Illuminates the Way

If there's one thing that can help spur executives into social action, it's good, old-fashioned data. Even today, there's still nothing quite like it. For this analysis, we asked Ann Charles, founder and CEO of BRANDfog, to comment on the rapid developments in executive culture, the challenges executives might face, and why social media makes for such an essential stepping stone.

For CEOs and social media, an irreversible power shift is under-way. Social networks made up of customers, investors, and other stakeholders are becoming stronger than the organizations they orbit, and these networks can impose their will. If social media can help topple corrupt governments, it can unseat unscru-pulous and unpopular CEOs. Today, real risk for corporations is more likely to originate from outside a company than from within.

Thus, the challenge for CEOs is to harness the power of social media and turn it to a leadership advantage. While a company's stock price was once the sole indicator of great leadership, there's now increased emphasis on CEO visibility and accessibil-ity, as well as agility in crisis management. Social media drives progress on these fronts, as it forces companies to become more transparent—both in what they communicate to the public and the amount of information disclosed. This transparency and immediacy is a transformational force for better leadership.

While social media is new, the nexus between communication and leadership is not. Many of the world's greatest leaders— from Winston Churchill to Martin Luther King to Steve Jobs—have been highly skilled communicators. Proficiency is necessary to inspire confidence in a CEO's vision and belief that he or she is taking the company in the right direction. Social media, in all its forms, empowers CEOs to improve communication skills, deepen connections with people inside and outside the company, and emerge as more effective leaders.

Data from BRANDfog's 2013 CEOs, Social Media and Leadership Survey

- How effective is it for CEOs to use Social Media to communicate company mission and values? 82.5 percent of respondents believe it is either very or somewhat effective.
- How effective is it for CEOs to use Social Media to attract new talent and implement employment branding? 80.9 percent of respondents believe it is either very or somewhat effective.
- How effective is it for CEOs to use Social Media to increase brand loyalty? 83.9 percent believe that CEO engagement on social media is somewhat or very effective for increasing brand loyalty, and only 16.1 percent believe it to be ineffective.
- How effective is it for CEOs to use Social Media to increase purchase intent? 80.8 percent of respondents believe it is either very or somewhat effective.

What Does It Mean to Be a Social Executive?

Much of the value the social executive brings to the table involves the flow of information. Traditional business models have prized the hierarchical structure, where ideas continue to be passed upward, expecting a decision to eventually be handed down. In social business, however, information often passes horizontally rather than vertically, empowering employees to better champion their own solutions to pressing questions rather than waiting idly by for an answer to come down from the top. According to Ben Edwards, Vice President of Global Communications and Digital Marketing at IBM, "These networks of expertise pass on information in amazingly fluid ways. Today, more often than not, the manager knows quite a bit less than the people they are managing around those horizontal flows of information."

Businesses need to be quicker with response times. Increased horizontal flexibility allows decisions to be made faster—and often by people better capable of making the right calls for the business. With top-down decision making becoming less important, the role of the social executive has become one of motivation and support, inspiring employees to follow their lead.

Brands continue to develop more nuanced relationships with employees and customers. The response from the business world has been to develop a new vernacular for the modern social executive. To be fair, businesses will always need decision makers and strong leaders, but the words we keep hearing to describe modern executives have become increasingly humanizing. Today, brands prize confident communicators in the C-Suite, leaders who represent a company's interests with honesty and transparency. In truth, these traits are no different from what has come to be expected from the entire workforce. Executives, however, have a special opportunity to inspire those traits in employees by modeling the behaviors in social media.

As mentioned earlier, executives are often reluctant to engage in social media either because they're unsure where to begin or because they lack the infrastructure to effectively incorporate social practices into their workdays. It is known that the role of social media will only increase over the next few years, but this transition is going to require leadership. The executive who steps into the social arena today will help shape the conversation, get ahead of the issues, and be able to address those issues long before becoming a problem.

Seven Personalities of a Social Executive

The idea of the social executive has been gaining steam for quite some time. As a result, much digital ink has been spilled on the subject. In Mark Fidelman's April 2012 piece for *Forbes*, he listed what he considered to be the most pervasive negative traits still present in many executives today.[6] We were captivated by the article, and in our exchanges with Fidelman, we decided that his article needed a companion piece; if the traits Fidelman listed in his blog post were antithetical to the spirit of social businesses, what traits would be the most valuable? Our answer to this question resulted in our Blue Focus Marketing blog post "7 Personalities of a Social Executive,"[7] which we have summarized here.

1: The Malleable Mind

Social executives don't feel threatened by change. They thrive in environments full of new ideas and innovative solutions. They don't expect the C-Suite to be the only hub of ideas or innovation either. Malleable Minds work to develop malleable cultures because it is understood a good idea won't be kept down for long. Further, the Malleable Mind doesn't let ego stand in the way of receiving feedback, and understands that respect is earned not through an iron fist, but through an open mind.

2: The Multilateral Boss

When we described the seven essential traits of the social employee in Chapter 4, one trait mentioned was being a born collaborator. The Multilateral Boss operates under the same assumption and understands that it doesn't matter where the best ideas come from, just that the right people hear them. Social businesses rely on crowdsourced collaboration in a variety of different ways, and the Multilateral Boss ensures that communication channels remain as open and accessible as possible.

3: The First-Hand Exec

First-Hand Execs like to roll up their sleeves and dive right in. Social media and the social business practices they facilitate cannot be understood through statistics and reports—they must be experienced. Social media demands immersive interaction. Because of this, First-Hand Execs won't let a lack of knowledge get the best of their curiosity. Learning social media is very much like learning a new language. As any foreign exchange student will say, you can take as many classes as you like, but the best way to truly learn is to go to the source and experience it yourself.

4: The Giraffe

The imagery here is unmistakable. The Giraffe is unafraid of sticking its neck out. Really, it's not about being afraid or unafraid. Giraffes stick their necks out because they can't help but do so—it's in their very nature. Executives are, by nature, a very visible part of the company they work for. They are obligated to represent the business with transparency and authenticity, regardless of whether responding to positive or negative feedback. A giraffe understands that to exist, there must be a level playing field. In the same respect, a social executive must understand that in order to level the field they play on, engagement must be authentic to establish trust and drive conversation. They are approachable, available, visible, and—most importantly—vulnerable.

5: The Master of the Ripple Effect

The "ripple effect" involves the way prominent voices resound in social media. Successful social executives know that what is said has an impact in the business world much in the same way a pebble has after being dropped in a still pond. In the same way, it is understood that priorities set for themselves and for their brand ripple through the workforce, helping to provide a common branding purpose. This top-down process drives social change by demonstrating the power of individuals leading by example and modeling the behaviors necessary for full social integration.

6: The Outside-In Exec

In Chapter 5, we talked about IBM and the growing need for brands to align internal identities with public identities. To attempt to do otherwise at a time when transparency is highly valued is a dangerous prospect at best, but potentially crippling for a brand's reputation at worst. The Outside-In Exec understands that social businesses have to mirror the outside world in the way they operate. Not only is this the best way to facilitate transparency, it's the best way to stay in touch with an ever-changing social landscape. The internal can't just reflect the external; it must try to reproduce it. Executives should always have one ear to the ground in order to learn from other businesses and leaders engaged in social media. The best ideas should be brought back to their own brands and repurposed.

7: The Information Circuit

In the same way trait 2 (the Multilateral Boss) understands the value of brainpower, the Information Circuit follows suit. These execs certainly aren't afraid of contributing their own ideas, but it is understood that every problem won't be solved independently. Above everything else within an organization, good ideas need to reach the ears of the right employees—the ones who can help make those ideas bloom into a reality. The Information Circuit happily poses questions to employees, collects responses, and forwards them along the path to actualization. This approach worked particularly well with Cisco's four-tiered conferencing channel during the company's Strategic Leader Exchange.

Recognizing Social Leadership— The #Nifty50 Top Men and Women on Twitter Awards

In 2011, we partnered with social entrepreneur Tom Pick and his Webbiquity blog to introduce the first annual #Nifty50 Top Men and Women on Twitter Awards. We designed the #Nifty50 as our way of recognizing the many social media early adopters in today's executive ranks. If the social employee of tomorrow is to flourish, we need to recognize the social leaders of today and offer the necessary resources to create effective cultural change agents.

Each year for the #Nifty50 Awards, we try to target a different group of people in order to put diverse industry sectors in the spotlight. In our inaugural year of 2011, we kept things a little looser with a general category. In 2012, we narrowed our focus specifically to honor leaders in the tech sector. For our 2013 awards, the spotlight will be placed on leading bloggers, writers, authors, and PR representatives. The constant shift in our focus is an attempt to show the value every sector of the business and marketing community brings to the table.

On the value of this project, our friend Tom Pick said:

> When you're an early adopter, it's too easy sometimes to feel like you're the only one walking against the grain into a new future. The #Nifty50 Awards bring social executives together to demonstrate both to them and the outside world that these leaders are part of a growing community. This in turn helps build a tremendous sense of camaraderie, where authentic relationships can be forged without anyone having to worry about ego or competitive edge. When the best thought leaders can share ideas in an open arena, everyone stands to benefit.

A tremendous response for these awards was received through the first two years of the program, with many recipients of the #Nifty50 Awards proudly displaying their badges on their blogs and social profiles. Our goal is to expand the program each year in new ways. Our most recent inclusion, #Nifty50 Kids, assists economically disadvantaged communities through technology donations to schools in need.

New Needs Call for New Roles

As things stand today, most brands don't need—or at least haven't created—a dedicated social media position in the C-Suite. However, with more and more of companies' operating budgets being dedicated to both internal and external social media engagement, executives will need to begin this conversation soon. While we have stressed in this chapter that all executives need to learn to be social regardless of title, their roles can be expanded or reimagined only so much.

There have been many ideas proposed by other experts in the field as to what may transpire. A 2011 post by Paul Hagen listed several of the common positions opening up on the executive level, including Chief Customer Officer, Chief Client Officer, and Chief Experience Officer.[8] These positions have clearly been designed with the idea of strengthening client and public engagement. As Dion Hinchcliffe noted, these executive positions are limited in that they're both customer-facing (and therefore ignoring internal social needs) and focused on public outreach in general instead of social media in particular.[9]

Hinchliffe proposed promoting the position of Chief Social Officer. This person would be "focused on where the company is heading in terms of how it operates and has control over engagement across all constituencies and stakeholders."[10] Such a position wouldn't be limited to improving public image through social media. Instead, the CSO would provide a big-picture vision of what a brand's social journey should look like and then map out the best routes to get there. The benefit of such an approach, according to Hinchcliff, is that the CSO would enable companies to focus on the impacts of social media on business, rather than simply on the technology itself.

Michael Brenner, Vice President of Marketing and Content Strategy at SAP and cofounder of Business2Community.com, believes that new executive or management positions should be driven based on a brand's social needs:

> *What I call "the Social Business imperative" is driving the creation of new roles to emerge in leading organizations. This is coming from the need to address the gap between the way our customers seek information during the buying process and the gaps in the information businesses and marketers are providing them.*

The roles that are being created include the Content Strategist and Chief Content Officer, Data Scientists in marketing who provide social and search-based analytics, and Social Business Managers who are social marketers that spread into other departments like sales and customer support to drive social media expertise. These roles will help companies to bridge the gaps and address the changing buyer journey. And they will do this by driving a social business focus on inside-out customer thinking.

Dedicated social positions in the C-Suite likely won't begin to seriously take right away. For so many brands, the social business conversation itself is a big enough first step, and so many will shy away from retooling positions at the executive level. However, as more money continues to be funneled into social media through either marketing or the development of enterprise technology, the need for a dedicated social expert at the highest levels of a company will be increasingly more apparent. Until that time, responsibility will largely have to be shared, with social CMOs emerging as de facto leaders.

The New CMO Is Social

While we wait to see what effect the rise of social business might have on the C-Suite, we asked our friend Vala Afshar, Chief Marketing Officer and Chief Customer Officer at Enterasys and winner of our 2012 #Nifty50 Top Twitter Men in Technology Award, to share the story of his own social journey:

> In a November 2012 post in the Wall Street Journal titled "Must-Have Job Skills in 2013," a research study revealed that personal branding is one of the four essential skills required by executives and business leaders. As stated by Meredith Haberfeld, an executive and career coach in New York, "More and more employers are looking for employees to tweet on their behalf, to blog on their behalf, to build an audience and write compelling, snappy posts."
>
> In the social era, employees have the unprecedented ability to either help or hurt a company's brand. Social collaboration

within business enables organizations to have greater visibility into our employee's judgment, influence, shared experiences, and knowledge. As Tom Peters so eloquently stated, "Brand equals talent." As a social business, you have to be able to recruit and keep the best talent, because today the employee is the brand. Perhaps in the past, only frontline employees in sales and services were best suited to represent the company brand, but with the advent and growth of social media, any employee has the opportunity to be seen or heard.

Recognizing the importance of networking and collaboration is exactly what led me to shift my focus to social media in 2011. I recognized that in the social era, customers have choices and voices with scales and amplitude, and therefore businesses need to transform and embrace social collaboration to meet the connected customer. The only way businesses can scale is to empower every single employee to collaborate and delight. In the case of Enterasys, I decided that I needed to set the example for social collaboration for the company. At that time, I was the Chief Customer Officer responsible for the company's global service and support function. As the Chief Customer Officer, I also recognized that collaboration would lead to better understanding of customer needs and future buying requirements. But more importantly, collaboration would lead to a deeper personal connection with each customer.

In a Harvard Business Review *post titled "Meet Your Company's New Chief Customer Officer," Fatemeh Khatibloo said, "I believe that customer intelligence leaders, with their deep and broad understanding of customers, are the natural choice to lead organizations along the path to true customer centricity. They are the future CCOs." I knew that collaboration and personal branding was an important step towards scaling the company's brand and reach. I also knew that broader understanding of customers and the market was a critical success factor for every single executive at Enterasys.*

In 2011, I started to engage my customers, partners, and employees via Twitter. I aggressively adopted a thought leadership communication strategy that involved sharing best practices and the latest news regarding business, technology, leadership, and services-related content. I was extremely accessible and active on social media. I also worked diligently to invite other employees, including executives of Enterasys, to participate on Twitter. In one year, I had established myself as a social media subject matter expert with multiple guest posts in well-known publications. The posts led to being offered a keynote presentation, being invited to analyst and technology conferences, and ultimately, a book titled The Pursuit of Social Business Excellence.

The success of building my personal brand led me to an unexpected opportunity. In 2012, after only one year of active social networking, I had established myself as the main storyteller within Enterasys. My personal awareness in the market, based on my social networks, had somehow turned me into the face of the company. That said, the Enterasys CEO decided that it was time to challenge me to take the role of the company's Chief Marketing Officer and the Chief Customer Officer. The rationale was simple: one of the most trusted leaders in the company, responsible for running an award-winning customer service and support organization, would be the best candidate to manage the marketing function. At the time, Enterasys had a Net Promoter Score of 80, which was an industry best. Who better to tell the story than the most socially active, and well-connected, executive in the company?

Today, Enterasys is outpacing the market and delighting customers while actively building a social ecosystem that consists of customer advocates. In 2012, our policy, "We are a social business; we care more," helped earn a place for Enterasys as one of the top places to work with Boston Business Journal and the Boston Globe.

I believe the role of human resources in a social business will be immensely important as far as shaping and maintaining company culture. Businesses must be able to recruit employees that demonstrate the right balance of IQ (intelligence) and EQ (emotional) to participate in social collaboration. The right balance of social aptitude and attitude does not mean hiring a group primarily composed of extroverts, but rather it means finding employees that exhibit humility and a passion for service. Employees must have an open mind, a beginner's mindset—they must be curious and prejudice-free. A social HR organization will adopt a hunter's mentality, networking proactively to recruit candidates with social currency and influence.

I believe the best employees are not looking for work; they're too busy changing the world. The most sought after talent may have their heads down, grinding and producing amazing work, but still finding the time to be social. Some might not even have an updated résumé, because deep down they know their next move will either be an internal promotion or an opportunity offered to them through their existing network of other accomplished and trusted advisors. A proactive, hunterlike mentality, instead of a farming mentality, will enable a social business to recruit the very best talent—a socially engaged and dynamic employee— into our business.

CHAPTER 13

Finding Education in the Social University

With great power comes great responsibility. Many figures and texts throughout history have uttered variations on this phrase, from Voltaire to Franklin D. Roosevelt, to the Bible, to *Amazing Spider-Man*. When establishing a social employee culture for a business, the age-old maxim should help guide every aspect of the process. Over half of the world's population is now 25 years old or younger.[1] This incoming group of digital natives will wield a tremendous amount of power on business practices in the next decade and beyond—but that power must be harnessed in order to produce the outcomes necessary for twenty-first -century businesses to remain competitive and relevant.

The rapid changes brought about over the past decade as a result of digital technologies and the corresponding cultural shifts have created a somewhat unique dynamic in business. Baby boomers and genXers have come to find that the models the business world relied on for decades are no longer relevant. The time to evolve has arrived, but unfortunately, as digital immigrants, many do not have the proper skill set or mindset to fully transition a brand. On the other side of the generational line, millennials have been entering the business ranks in ever-increasing numbers. For many, if not most, their digital social networking skills have become ingrained in their daily routines. That being said, most lack the training and real-life experiences to properly leverage that know-how toward producing the desired business results. This chapter explores this new generational dynamic and the ways a strong digital/social education can teach social employees how to wield their power effectively and responsibly, whether at a university or in the workplace.

The Education Paradox

We asked our friend and expert analyst Mark Fidelman for his thoughts on social business education within the university system and how businesses can help support social education in order to produce a new generation of workers equipped with the business savvy necessary to go along with their built-in strengths as digital natives. As Fidelman pointed out, the majority of people understand how social networks can be used for personal situations, but managing those networks in a business context can present new challenges. Support in the educational system could dramatically ease this concern. However, to date, that support doesn't appear to be forthcoming:

> *I discovered during my extensive research that our best universities are not yet teaching their students how to use social media in a business framework. Universities (even the best) tend to be conservative, and as a consequence they are teaching business models that are less relevant. That will change as employers demand a more socially proficient workforce, but for now the responsibility resides with the organization.*

The dynamic that Fidelman observed creates a bit of a paradox. Traditionally, students gain their foundational knowledge of business operations through rigorous course work in the university system. While there, it is learned how most companies structure and equip themselves with the best practices to keep adopted processes running smoothly. For the most part, this process worked just fine throughout the twentieth century. However, the accelerated change in the curve of social business has created the need for an entirely new kind of knowledge base—one that university curriculum has so far either ignored or been unable to keep up with.

The problem isn't a matter of training, but of retraining. The success stories that have been explored in this book have demonstrated the value of in-house social media training for social employees. After all, every business has unique needs. Employees should expect specialized training when first entering a company's workforce. The problem arises when employers have to rebuild their employees from the ground up—training them to unlearn many of the "essential" concepts they learned in college. If the current educational system doesn't change, more and more employers will find they are dedicating far too many resources to reeducating incoming employees before being able to establish a common starting point.

Dropping Out and Plugging In

At the very least, such a dynamic carries inefficiencies, a fact that has not been lost on young professionals entering the workplace. The incoming millennial generation isn't content with just performing rote work for the sake of the task. They crave a deeper connection with the work performed, and many will disengage the moment they realize that connection isn't being satisfied. The following quote from Don Tapscott is an excerpt from Jacob Morgan's book *The Collaborative Organization*:

> *The baby boomers were satisfied with knowing what decision was made, but today's young employees want to know why. They're not insubordinate; they just recognize that understanding the reasons behind the decision can make the difference between success and failure in implementation.*[2]

As was seen in Chapter 8, companies such as Cisco not only prize the drive for the *why*, they make it a foundational element of their social business policies. Today's digital natives have a built-in set of skills perfectly suited for the social age. They know their skills are valuable, though perhaps a little unrefined. Unfortunately, when faced with curriculum that fails to even address this skill set—let alone provide them with a *why*—many millennials are simply choosing to skip the university system entirely and jump straight into the business world. This trend has become so prevalent that many smaller companies and start-ups have begun targeting this new class of workers, who show up at their new jobs wearing their collegiate drop-out status as badges of pride.[3]

Solutions on the Horizon

The social employees who choose the workforce over the university aren't necessarily making a bad decision. More than anything, they're being pragmatic by cutting out an inefficiency—and in the process, modeling a value very much prized in social business. What's the point of earning a degree if none of the skills gained have practical applications? Asking for the *why* in this way works as a form of self-preservation for millennials entering the workforce. To gain a competitive edge in a crowded employee pool, there is no choice but to seek the utility value in every task or assignment presented so as not to waste time on dead-end endeavors.

The university system at large may not be rising to meet the expectations of today's pragmatic, information-driven social employees, but that doesn't mean solutions aren't beginning to appear on the horizon. The Rutgers Center for Management Development (CMD) now offers a global suite of "Mini-MBA" programs that combine the best of academics and expert practitioners.

Eric Greenberg, Managing Director at the CMD, has acknowledged the challenges higher education faces as the business landscape begins to change. Greenberg recognized the critical need for the CMD to provide students with the necessary skills and background to succeed in a fast-paced digital world. As a result, Rutgers became one of the first major universities to offer executive education courses in digital marketing and social media. Said Greenberg, "Our program combines the academic rigor of a university with the practical skills and knowledge that executives can apply immediately back at their desks."

Universities like Rutgers understand that, if change is the only constant in an environment, a business curriculum must be based on change as well in order to adapt alongside the marketplace. For example, the Rutgers CMD offers a customized program in Strategic Healthcare Management that the school cobrands with a company. David Finegold, Rutgers SVP for Lifelong Learning and Strategic Growth, stated, "This program enables healthcare providers to build skills and to deliver the program in their context. Investing in your people shows the company's commitment."

Ultimately, commitment at such a level can manifest itself by producing empowered and engaged employees. Programs that offer a hands-on experience for students in a structured environment and foster learning and experimentation will eventually pay off in dramatic real-world results.

Training Is the Key to Retention

Why does having a solid educational foundation matter so much to businesses? It all comes down to achieving desired outcomes. As more brands learn to adopt social business models, the need for incoming employees to at least have a working knowledge of what these models look like will be a must. An incoming employee expecting a rigid, hierarchical model where information travels up and decisions travel down might have difficulty adjusting to the horizontal collaboration structures of a social business.

Fortunately, the American Marketing Association (AMA) has begun taking steps that help drive innovation in education. According to Nancy Costopulos, Chief Marketing Officer at the AMA, "By offering marketing workshops on topics ranging from integrated marketing communications and social media to content marketing, the AMA is working to bridge gaps in education and keep marketers ahead of the curve." Such programs help provide educational bridges that empower social employees of all ages and backgrounds. Anyone can learn to do things in new ways, but the motivation to do so must come from an established foundation of critical thinking.

With a solid foundation, the social graduate will better understand the *why* of the social business. Graduates will enter the workforce as converts ready to contribute immediately as evangelists in the community. Further, employees already comfortable with the theoretical underpinnings of social business practices will offer considerable resources not only to the brand at large, but also to coworkers. For instance, social graduates can help reverse mentor digital immigrants in management and the C-Suite, thereby increasing their own visibility within the company, and simultaneously demonstrate the value of social tools.

Of course, the ultimate beneficiary of aligning curriculum with internal brand training is the customer. Craig Hanna, EVP of North America at Econsultancy, likened effective training to a lightning rod for enhancing an employee's ability to engage customers in their preferred social channels. However, Hanna was also quick to offer a word of caution: "We need to remember that social technologies are only enablers—true success comes from using new social tools to build deeper relationships." In order to achieve success, brands must be prepared to combine effective training with a comprehensive company policy if they hope to successfully empower employees on behalf of the brand.

We have often spoken about the value of establishing an essential foundation from the earliest possible stages of planning a social business in order to create a transparent, unified front at every level. The social brand can provide something of value to the public by way of useful products and services, and in return, the public feeds back into the Möbius loop of interaction through valuable education and training.

Hinchcliffe: What Should Organizations Change to Accelerate Social Business?

Chapter 14 explores the different tools and methods used to build a thriving community of shared interest. If proper education and training form a pathway toward aligning the social business goals a brand has with the goals of the employees, the thriving communities will be the reward at the end of the road. To help shed more light on the essential mindsets brands and employees must have to adopt social success, we'd like to focus on the words of our colleague, Dion Hinchcliffe, Chief Strategy Officer at the Dachis Group:

> There are numerous reasons businesses are adopting social media more slowly than they might like. Of these, one of the more challenging issues is employing the medium so it's effective at driving useful business results. It's rather ironic that the key concerns are actually intrinsic to the very nature of social media itself—a highly open, participative, and self-organizing nature. This tends to rub against the grain of the hierarchical methods used to organize enterprises. A quick glance at the organizational chart of any business makes it clear: it looks far different than any visualization of a social network, with its egalitarian connections, free-form nature, and seeming lack of central control.

> The central question then is this: how can a business move beyond an intrinsic nature of over controlling business environments to adapt the benefits of social media to business? Clearly there is plenty of value to be had, the reported results of which turn up in survey after survey. In-depth analysis from many different sources can be seen, including McKinsey & Company, AIIM, IBM, and Frost and Sullivan, to name just a few. Are organizations so different from the general public that the benefits of connecting with each other via social networks don't work? And what about getting things done in ways that are easier, simpler, and richer than older models of communication?

As it turns out, unfortunately, businesses are indeed quite a bit different from open networks of people in the online world. There is a real tension between the controlled world of business and the social world of the online community. These two worlds were certainly not made for each other.

However, the news isn't all bad either. Evidence is mounting that the traditonal ways of thinking about organizational boundaries, such as departments, teams, and even the edges of our organization, are actually rather parochial. What's more, some organizations are getting past this point and figuring out how to apply social media to business with as little alteration as possible. When this occurs, the value received is substantially higher. Further, it is probably safe to say the value is large enough to have serious competitive consequences for some organizations that are late to adopt. To validate, the following represents numbers that have not yet been seen.

In a survey conducted by the Dachis Group Social Business Council during the summer of 2012, an interesting find was made. It was discovered that organizations look at social media through two very different lenses. The first lens is the world of the worker, where social media is used within the company to improve collaboration and information sharing among workers. The second lens is the one of external engagement with the world, such as marketing, sales, and customer care. This isn't new, but what was surprising was the degree to which these two worlds of social media were disconnected. Ninety-six percent of organizations surveyed in the council did not have a connection between their internal and external social media efforts at all.

This was a concern for several reasons. The most significant reason was a momentous finding that McKinsey & Company made in late 2011. Nearly 3,000 large organizations surveyed on the perceived benefits of the usage of social technology revealed that a leading edge minority were seeing particularly outsized benefits. The same minority also stood out for another reason.

The minority had a strong correlation with not establishing artificial boundaries among social environments. The environments that saw the most substance (and double-digit) benefits to customer-facing, workforce-facing, and supplier-facing functions had a fully networked ecosystem with as few boundaries as possible. The two lenses were connected. In other words, the companies that were outperforming other social businesses by a large margin did not artificially create silos of communication. Instead, social communication was allowed which enabled the accumulation of information from the point of origin to where it was needed with a minimal amount of friction and effort.

The council data showed that although organizations were busy trying to incorporate new social efforts, the same traditional barriers were being erected which inhibited change. The two lenses were not being fused to create a single ecosystem. Now, there is mounting evidence that this sharply constrains the value of social media for most organizations. The big lesson learned was social media must be looked at as a way to break down the unneeded barriers of communication that are actually preventing higher levels of business performance. Our legacy communication technologies had the same types of barriers. For this reason, social media warped into the old models tends to not deliver more than minor incremental value. Organizations need to learn from social media while adhering to the minimum necessary level of control over intellectual property, trade secrets, customer privacy, and other factors that simply can't be compromised. The message here is basic: truly open and participative organizations see higher value from social media. Those that aren't, don't. The lesson here is to be very, very careful not to re-erect the barriers of the old way of working in the era of social media.

CHAPTER 14

Building Communities
of Shared Interest

The famous business thinker Peter F. Drucker once declared, "The purpose of a business is to create a customer." This simple yet powerful statement has rightfully stood the test of time. It's hard to argue with such a tenet; without customers, what good are a brand's products and services? We all depend on customers to provide meaning and value to our work, even if we can sometimes lose sight of this fact when we're "huddled in the trenches," so to speak.

As we have argued throughout this book, the rules for acquiring and retaining customers in the new era of social business have changed. With the proliferation of social media tools, the customer's voice has never been stronger—driving a brand's image and reputation through intricate networks of influence. With this new dynamic in mind, Shiv Sing, Global Head of Digital for PepsiCo Beverages, recently amended Drucker's famous declaration by stating, "The purpose of a business is to create a customer . . . who creates customers."[1]

The relationship a brand establishes with its community is its most valuable social currency. Companies will live or die based on their ability to nurture these communities and activate loyal brand ambassadors around their messages. The idea of building energized relationships is built right into the DNA of social media. Yet, as we've said, a brand must strengthen its communities internally before it can succeed externally. In this chapter we will explore what it means for social employees to build communities of shared interest and the tools they can utilize to produce real results. To help us with this discussion, we have enlisted the expert advice of several social business thought leaders who have our deepest respect within the industry.

Trends of the Day in Employee Brand Ambassadorship

Social employees may leverage social media tools as individuals, but it must always be remembered that they are operating under the umbrella of their brands. As such, these employees may be afforded a great deal of freedom in how they move through the digital bazaar, but those movements must align with their brand's mission, vision, and values. If social employees can act responsibly on behalf of their brand, they will be able to successfully leverage their communities to create meaningful—and useful—engagement opportunities.

In order for the social employee's own activities to line up with the brand's goals, brands must first be able to engage their employees internally, activating them around a common purpose with established goals and a basic framework for executing them. We asked our colleague Fred Burt, Director of European Clients at Interbrand, about some of the challenges many brands face as they work to establish this framework:

> With my larger clients, I'm seeing a real tension. On the one hand, they need to manage the brand centrally in order to ensure some sort of coherence across multiple business units, offers, media, and customer types. On the other, the day-to-day decision making often takes place in the businesses and away from the central teams. So it's imperative that the central brand team finds a means to engage with their internal stakeholders and creates ways in which to facilitate active participation in what the brand can mean for them.

Brands Ride Shotgun in Social Networks

The idea of missing out plays a central role in social media engagement. As we said in Chapter 1, conversations about brands are taking place on social media whether the brand is involved or not. In this way, every company's social journey has already begun. Because of this, brands need to remember that although it's essential for employees to represent their companies in these social forums, they will only meet resistance if they try to control the interactions too forcefully. We asked Scott Davis, Chief Growth Officer at Prophet, an international strategic brand and marketing consultancy, to expand this idea a little further:

> *The best companies and brands have learned that they need to leverage other assets to do some of the heavy lifting for them. For instance, the moms at Procter & Gamble do all the heavy lifting on all the market research. This "mom blog" world does the pushing for P&G, making it much more targeted to the people who buy the brand.*

Businesses may not be in the driver's seat the way they used to be, but that doesn't mean they can't go along for the ride. Today's businesses ride shotgun on the social journey. They may not have direct control over their journey anymore, but they're the trusted navigators, the extra pair of eyes looking down the road for any hidden obstacles. When community members are allowed to help set the agenda when it comes to a brand's products and priorities, deeper connections between brand, customer, and community are created.

Picking the Right Social Platforms

At this point in the book, we've spent a good deal of time extolling the virtues of social media and how it can improve the working experience of the employee of the twenty-first century. However, we've spent far less time actually speaking about specific social media tools, their functions, and their value to businesses.

Our reasons for this are twofold: first, the big names in the social media game are always changing, and any attempt on our part to list these platforms in a book runs the risk of appearing dated even a year down the road. Second, every brand will have different social media needs. The platforms and tools that work best for a Fortune 500 multinational corporation will naturally be different from the ones employed by a hot new Silicon Valley start-up.

Our friend David Brier, President and Creative Director of DBD International, stressed that brands must learn to develop or adopt the platforms that make the most sense for their business needs and brand voice. Having enough viable options isn't the problem— new social media tools are popping up by the day. The important thing is that employees master the tools their companies do choose to use. "To me, the best way to do this is to take it one tool at a time," Brier said. "Trying to master everything at once will only lead to confusion."

While far from comprehensive, the following platforms offer a glimpse into how businesses both large and small are utilizing specialized social media platforms to perform a variety of tasks, from customer relations management (CRM) to task management, public engagement to influence tracking. As of this writing, these tools are ranked among the most popular platforms. We acknowledge that in an era of extreme change, a comparable list could look very different a few years down the road.

Important Tools for Collaboration and Community Building

IBM Connections (see Chapter 5). Connections was developed in-house as a way of managing IBM's own social business needs. It facilitates customer relationship management and internal communication and collaboration, as well as external sharing. Connections was designed to integrate all the daily activities of a social employee into a single platform in order to streamline productivity and access to information.

Salesforce. The cloud-based Salesforce platform operates as an all-in-one platform much like IBM's Connections, making the two platforms the current industry leaders in comprehensive enterprise social business operations. Like many social management platforms, Salesforce is designed to integrate and utilize information from a variety of different accounts, including Google and Microsoft Outlook. The benefit of this approach is that social employees have access to all their information on a single, consolidated platform. Salesforce's Chatter feature also allows for easy communication and collaboration across employee networks. Salesforce's Radian6 social media monitoring tool allows companies to track conversations about their brand and other keywords on social platforms. Through this social listening tool, businesses can learn who its brand influencers are, what is being said about the company, and how these conversations are taking shape over time.

Nimble. Nimble is a Social Relationship Management CRM tool designed to help individuals and teams develop their personal brand, nurture business relationships, and work together as a team to turn social conversations into customers. This is accomplished by automatically combining a team's business contacts, social conversations, and emails into one simple cloud-based solution. Businesses can then foster relationships with potential clients through the various social media channels they employ. Through this service, employees can communicate with a client across multiple platforms, and assign tasks related to that client to other team members. Nimble's recent partnership with HootSuite (discussed later) allows for a "closed-loop" process of listening, monitoring, and engagement that has further enhanced the value and flexibility of the platform.

Yammer/Jive Software/SAP Streamwork/Microsoft Sharepoint.
These platforms allow team members to manage projects, collaborate, and edit files in real time. Sortable features within these platforms update members on the status of specific tasks and files, keeping employees apprised on the progress of specific projects, even if they're not actively working on them. Employees can easily alert coworkers or other work groups to useful content through "@" messages, or invite them to collaborate on new projects. Platforms like Streamwork and Sharepoint offer data analysis tools to help employees and groups make more informed decisions, and Sharepoint also offers full integration with Microsoft's Office Suite.

Basecamp. This project management platform works wonders for keeping teams updated and on task—especially when expected to juggle multiple projects at once. Through the easy creation of task lists, project managers can assign responsibilities and deadlines to various team members. Every task created has its own separate window for dialogue and file sharing, eliminating the tedium of searching through endless comment threads for information.

Google+ Communities. Google enhanced their Google+ social networking site to include a feature called Communities. This tool enables users to build communities of any size, create events, start hangouts and discussions, and share content. This tool enables social employees to engage and network with customers, and begin conversations with prospects. Businesses can use the Communities feature to create private or public communities, presenting an opportunity for employees to become thought leaders on important industry topics.

Triberr. In this world of content as cultural currency, Triberr offers brands the ability to distribute content across multiple social channels. This innovative social platform builds thought leadership and influencers by tapping into networks of engaged communities. Triberr offers several other unique features that rise above and beyond mere content distribution:

- ▶ Next Generation Syndication Capabilities: Ability to republish a blog post along with content, links, authorship, and comments section.
- ▶ Triberr PRIME. A premium set of socially-centric features that will replace RSS and email marketing, enable users to grow larger tribes, automate sharing for highly trusted content creators, and more.
- ▶ Powerful Influencer Marketing Campaigns: Dozens of influential bloggers collaborating to promote a product or brand.

HootSuite/Tweetdeck/Buffer. Any social employee active on platforms such as Twitter, LinkedIn, or Facebook can dramatically streamline their posting process with automated posting platforms like HootSuite, Tweetdeck, or Buffer. These services were created to help employees share content across multiple social networks through a single centralized hub. Scheduling features within these programs allow content producers to expand their reach by posting at peak hours; spread posts out over days, weeks, or months; and reduce the time spent switching from network to network.

Klout/Kred. These tools allow users to monitor social employee influence, networks, and engagement across multiple platforms. Through their respective analytics matrixes, Kred and Klout track a user's posts on different platforms and then rate those posts based on the level of engagement (e.g. click or comments) that those posts produce. Users can also learn about their influence on specific platforms as a percentage of their total social presence, what types of posts generate the most buzz, and what members of their community are consistently the most engaged.

The Value of Employee Branding, Social Influence, and Social Currency

As the saying goes, each of us is a unique snowflake setting out on a path wholly unique to ourselves. As unique as each of us may be, we don't exist in a vacuum—we are rarely, if ever, the only snowflakes tumbling through the sky. We each play our own roles, but it's the cumulative result of millions of snowflakes falling over a quiet winter's night that produces the real impact for brands. Social businesses behave much like falling snow, amplifying the trajectories of countless individuals to develop a rich, pervasive presence, one that is remarkable for its complexity and character at the group and individual levels.

For further insight about the cumulative effect that individual efforts can have for a company's social presence online, we spoke with Andreas Ramos, Digital Marketing Practice Leader at the CMO Council and author of multiple books including *Search Engine Marketing* and most recently *The Big Book of Content Marketing* (andreas. com, 2013). According to Ramos, social activity has an interesting way of building on itself—the more links and pages a brand can produce about its products and services, the higher it will rank in search engines and the more traffic it will generate. Blog posts and tweets that link back to the company will also produce a greater impact in addition to presenting a unified message to consumers.

Ramos added that the results of these efforts can be quantified as well, noting that each employee should have a personal tracking tag to add to his or her links. Web analytics can show the leads and sales from those links. Nevertheless, brands should exercise discretion about what they post. "Employees should also be careful in talking about strategies or upcoming products," Ramos said. "Competitors can easily find and review all blogs and tweets by a company's staff and family to gain insider information or measure sentiment."

Communities thrive on the contributions of the individual, but brands that unify their social employees under a common set of practices will benefit tremendously from the complex, sticky relationships that develop from such contributions. With the proper system in place, brands can ensure that each contribution points community members in the same direction—back to the brand. Further, these results can be easily measured to determine which individual's contributions are generating the greatest impact. Once a brand has identified its greatest contributors, it should seek not only to reward those efforts, but also to learn how they can serve as models of success for everyone else.

The Value of Social Currency

With a continued pattern of individual contribution and engagement, both social employees and the brands they represent begin to build a great deal of cultural capital, or as Erich Joachimsthaler, CEO of Vivaldi Partners Group, called it, "social currency." Joachimsthaler said, "Our research with over 7,000 consumers in the U.S. and Europe shows that the impact of social currency can be measured on consideration, purchase, and loyalty."[2]

Social currency, Joachimsthaler said, manifests itself in a number of ways. But, he stressed that any attempt to build up a cache must be based on the assumption that our lives are fundamentally social. Working off this assumption, employee branding can be especially effective in environments where the employees are directly linked up with a company's customers. Joachimsthaler used Best Buy's "Twelpforce" initiative to illustrate. In that program, Best Buy encouraged every employee to sign up for a "Twelp" (tweet + help) account, which allowed consumers to ask a staff of about 2,000 employees any sales, technical, or product-related questions and get immediate responses. "This program encouraged the Twelpforce to compete to answer each question as quickly as possible, which built Best Buy's brand reputation for responsiveness and created significant employee engagement by employees,"[3] Joachimsthaler said.

That example expertly showed how a group of dedicated individuals can contribute to a larger goal through small efforts. Not every employee is expected to answer every question that's posed to the brand, but as long as each individual gives time to answer at least a few questions each day the system works in perpetuity. Further, by adding a plurality of voices, Best Buy ensures that customers will always be put in contact with the right person for the question. This democratization of service empowers employees by allowing a broad range of individuals to contribute, but the real benefit to the process lies in the public perception of the program. Customers who witness their questions are being seen and answered quickly and accurately by a large group of dedicated professionals will reward these brands with increased loyalty and social advocacy.

Employee Voices and Your Brand

Never before has the individual employee voice been able to resonate on a scale that somehow manages to be both granular in its appeal and yet global in its reach. Once a community of social employees has been activated around a brand's mission, vision, and values, brand visibility will expand in both reach and dimension. Brands must recognize the potential of social media to facilitate this process. According to Charlene Li at Altimeter Group, brands must be willing to view their employees in a positive light, rather than as "potential social media time bombs that could go off without warning."[4]

This isn't to say that risk isn't part of the social business process. Employees working under the umbrella of a brand need to know where their personal brand ends and their employer's brand begins. Brands must be careful to establish these protocols immediately or risk losing the communities their employees built on the company's behalf. To explore this idea further, we asked Meghan M. Biro, founder and CEO of TalentCulture Consulting Group and the TalentCulture World of Work Community to share her thoughts with us:

> Brands big and small see the value of allowing employees with strong social presences to become brand ambassadors. Some brands empowering employee brand ambassadors see fault lines developing—chief among which is who owns the brand, the employee-as-brand-ambassador, or the company?
>
> Best Buy is a recent example of brand-owner social media conflict. Its former CEO, Brian Dunn, and CMO, Barry Judge, used Twitter extensively under the handles @BBYCEO and

@BestBuyCMO. Both left the company in spring 2012, changing their Twitter handles to @BrianDunn and @BarryJudge. Immediately Best Buy lost access to the roughly 37,000 Twitter followers of Judge and Dunn—a huge blow that Forbes *contributor Ann Charles likened to having 37,000 customers opt out of email databases.*[5]

In the aftermath, both executives were locked out of Best Buy Twitter accounts; the company tried to establish the interim CEO as the new @BBYCEO persona, a clumsy move which saw followers drop from 15,000 to slightly over 500. More was lost than Twitter followers—Best Buy also lost its investment in building a trusted conversation with customers using the CEO's Twitter presence.

Few C-suite occupants are Twitter habitués. Nevertheless the Best Buy example is a stark lesson of the potential risks in conflating personal and corporate brands. While it may seem obvious that a company owns its brand on social media channels, there is a need to balance the benefits and opportunities offered by employee brand ambassadors against the risks of brand dilution and lack of control of company messages (and followers). Spreading the risk is one solution—encouraging the empowerment of many company brand ambassadors on social media channels reduces the risk of a sudden falloff in influence if one or two leave the company.

Goals›Processes›Plans

Making it simple for brand ambassadors to represent a company while ensuring messages are consistent without losing brand ownership is more difficult than it may seem. High-profile brand ambassadors like Dunn and Judge surely drew more followers through their status in the company than would an employee of less status. This underscores the need to set a border between the company's brand and the individual's by building a bigger pool of ambassadors and by creating a brand ambassador process guide, complete with succession planning. The guide should not only include dos and don'ts for employees who choose to represent the company via social media; it should give the company the ability to manage the ambassador/brand identity gap.

Appropriate Process, Intelligent Control = Training

It's also a brand's responsibility to ensure followers aren't confused by multiple personas with slightly different perspectives or stories. Control of a brand extends to well-understood and disseminated corporate messages, appropriate hashtags, and commenting recommendations.

Managing the Employee Brand Ambassador

Many millenials and genXers have developed personal brands across a variety of social media channels. They may feel this investment should be rewarded by the company, either in salary, bonuses, or freedom to maintain personal brands during work hours. This can create problems with peers who may not be as socially active. For example, rewards may be expected, but difficult to administer without alienating someone. People may decline to be brand ambassadors, yet resent those who are compensated for taking on the task. Transparency is your ally: if someone is a brand ambassador, create productivity/billability goals appropriate to your organization.

Managing Culture Change

Brand ambassadors using social channels force culture change on brands. Assess the cultural impact of brand ambassadors by measuring brand stability and/or change caused by brand ambassadors. Social media measurement takes the pulse of an organization and provides a health check, not only of the brand but also of employee attitudes and engagement.

Social media presence is critical to brand development and customer engagement. It's smart to encourage employees to be brand ambassadors, and necessary to create processes to protect both ambassadors and the brand. Social media is a maturing practice. With social media process and policy, you'll have both a strong brand and engaged brand ambassadors.

CHAPTER 15

How Content Marketing Empowers Social Employees

Today's brands have content marketing on their minds. This rapidly proliferating social strategy has become all the rage in both B2B and B2C communities, and it's not hard to see why. The currency of the empowered consumer is content—helpful how-to videos, interviews with industry thought leaders, incisive blog posts—and marketers are falling over themselves to get in on the action.

What makes content marketing so powerful? Where do we start? Content marketing fosters conversations, not monologues. It inspires engagement, not impatience. It builds communities, not faceless customers.

Content marketing, in other words, is not your grandfather's marketing strategy.

Great content is contagious. It can engage interested customers at any point in the buying process. Content marketing may just be the most valuable social engagement tool that brands have available to them—and its power is just beginning to be tapped. Brands building toward a social future must be prepared to arm employees with compelling, dynamic content in order to build an online presence and keep buyers engaged.

Getting from Point A to Point B

Social media has dramatically expanded the amount of touch points available to marketers. Brands are moving from traditional channels like radio, television, or print, and are learning to craft messages to fit the ever-growing number of social platforms available on the web. Content marketing is not a one-size-fits-all venture; different approaches work for different mediums. On Twitter, marketers have 140 characters to figure out how to engage readers. On LinkedIn, brand ambassadors can build influence on discussion boards and thought leader channels in order to facilitate deeper engagement. Brands operating on multiple platforms have a responsibility to learn the rules of each new environment, and adjust their content campaigns accordingly. As Carolin Probst-Iyer, Manager of Digital Consumer Engagement at Chevrolet, said:

> You can't just decide one day you want to do content marketing. Strategy plays an important role. Go out and see whom you are trying to reach, what are their passion points and what are the stories and messages you want to convey as a brand. Then choose your tactics.[1]

At Blue Focus Marketing, we have designed and delivered numerous workshops for the American Marketing Association that are centered on content marketing and integrated marketing communications (another hot topic of the day). The workshops focus a great deal on content marketing strategy. Anyone can produce content—and in fact more and more people, whether amateurs or professionals, are doing so each day. Going in without a strategy is akin to going in blind. As we've said repeatedly throughout this book, brands may not need to know every nuance of a platform before diving in, but that's no excuse for going in with a half-baked approach. Marketers can learn plenty of new tricks along the way—but they have to have a cohesive strategy in place to develop the proper tools and set out on the right path.

Strategy is all about getting from point A to point B, or from where you are today to where you want to be tomorrow. The properly executed strategy turns obstacles into opportunities, helping marketers create connections between the brand and the audience. Social employees make for the ideal content delivery agents, building meaningful interactions with customers through their dynamic presentations of information.

Building a Winning Content Strategy

First, consider your brand's value proposition (BVP). What are the fundamental reasons people choose your brand versus alternatives? Starting with the BVP, the brand's story can then be crafted by determining what the brand stands for in the minds of the target audience. If the true strength of the brand can be identified, valuable insight will be gained as to what your key messages should become. A powerful content strategy enhances a marketer's ability to deliver brand messages across multiple touch points. Brands capable of delivering a consistent message and persona regardless of where content is being delivered will have a considerable leg up on the competition in building engaged communities.

A winning content strategy doesn't just target customers, however. The viral nature of social media demands that brands find allies during the quest to distribute content as far and wide as possible. To do this, marketers must include any and all prominent influencers in their immediate circle. Without these key players to champion content and redistribute it, a social employee's reach could end up becoming severely limited. The best content benefits from having multiple sources rallying around it, each providing a unique spin on the information. Stakeholders should include industry experts, bloggers, PR professionals, social media professionals, business partners, employees, and—perhaps most importantly—customers in the marketplace.

"I Helped Put a Man on the Moon"

There's an old story that often gets told about a visit President John F. Kennedy once made to NASA. While walking the halls of the young space program, the President came across a cleaner and struck up a conversation. Casually, Kennedy asked the man what his job was at NASA. The cleaner smiled and replied, "My job is to help put a man on the moon."

As it turns out, the story itself might be a fabrication, an inspirational tale told to embody the ideals of the time. But its message is unmistakable. The story teaches that at NASA, every employee was united in a common goal—they were literally shooting for the moon. While most people would look at the man and see a lowly wage worker in a menial job, he saw himself as a part of a history-making event, and he was correct for doing so. This tale illustrates perfectly the power of a brand's mission, vision, and values. With every employee that buys in, the organization is stronger for it.

A brand's vision, the very essence of its story, must be embodied in its content marketing message. At their very best, slogans can embody the essence of these messages and serve a higher purpose aside from just being memorable. As Scott Davis, Chief Growth Officer at Prophet, said, it can "ignite employees." These slogans extend far beyond simple concepts of products and services, and speak directly to the brand's core values. IBM is working toward a "Smarter Planet," Coca-Cola strives for "Happiness," and Apple encourages us to "Think Different." GE has championed eco-imagination, while State Farm wants its customers to live confidently.

At the Cleveland Clinic, it's all about "Patients First." In a 2012 interview, CEO Toby Cosgrove said, "'Patients First' isn't just a slogan at Cleveland Clinic; it's our guiding principle. That is where we get our satisfaction and our motivation."[2] This foundational mindset must be present in the way a brand operates. A slogan has to flow organically from the company's mission, and it must be an instantly recognizable embodiment of a brand's story. If it isn't, if the slogan somehow rings falsely in the ears of consumers, brands will face a credibility gap between the story they're trying to tell and the story they're actually telling.

Stories Turn Your Brand into a Friend, Worthy of Trust

Content marketing federalizes responsibility for the brand. No longer is promoting the brand and its story exclusive to the marketing department—social business has made this everyone's job. In content marketing, social employees invite customers along for a ride. Dynamic engagement sets the stage for an infinite number of possible outcomes, which are limited only by the imaginations of customers, contributors, and co-collaborators.

The brands most successful at relating to their customers will benefit tremendously in earned cultural capital. The more cultural capital a brand can build, the more forgiveness it will have earned whenever it eventually takes the occasional (and unavoidable) misstep. By default, every social employee with a presence on social platforms represents their brand, and as such they have a responsibility to present their brand's vision with authenticity and consistency. Content marketing may be everyone's job, but it's the marketing department's job to ensure social employees are well equipped with the right tools and information necessary to make an impact.

All of this starts with telling a strong story. As stated by Melinda Partin in her *Fast Company* article:

> *The goal with corporate-brand storytelling is to transition the consumer from awareness to trial to advocacy. You want people to use your brand to describe their life: a "Windows User," a "Mac Guy," a "Honda driver" and so on. Once the consumer adopts a product into his or her personal story, brand exposure increases greatly.*[3]

Content marketing provides a dynamic platform for developing this kind of steadfast brand loyalty. However, brands can't just start throwing random content against the wall to see what sticks. They have to know what it is about their brands that customers identify with, and build their stories around that.

Content Marketing Success Story: Chipotle

It's becoming easier and easier to find sterling examples of successful content marketing campaigns that have enriched brand value in the public eye. One especially popular example within the last couple years is the "Back to the Start" video created by Chipotle Mexican Grill in 2011.[4] The animated video expertly relates the brand's story through its values—prizing organic, sustainable farming and animal husbandry practices over the more common factory farming approaches. While not everyone may agree with that message, the video has an unmistakable emotional core, and its message is hard to confuse.

http://www.youtube.com/watch?v=aMfSGt6rHos

The video had originally been intended as a humble YouTube post, something Chipotle could point the public toward as a handy way of showing what it stood for. But then a funny thing happened: people started sharing it. Suddenly it began winning awards and generating discussion. It even ended up on TV as the brand's first national commercial, though the brand had certainly never originally conceived of gaining such exposure. As of this writing, the video has over 7 million views on YouTube, a shining example of how good content marketing can activate its base around a good story.

One essential strength of the message is what our friend Simon Mainwaring calls "contributory consumption," the idea that most customers like to know they are "doing good" through their purchase decisions.[5] Chipotle incorporates this idea of social progress through responsible farming right into the heart of its story, preparing the way for deeper relationships with both employees and customers. As Andy Smith, coauthor of *The Dragonfly Effect*, wrote on his blog, "We know that consumers want you to stand for something. It doesn't have to be breast cancer, poverty, or hunger. It can be as simple as food with integrity."[6]

Components of a Good Story

Now that we've established the value in effective content marketing through storytelling, let's break down the essential components of a good story. What is it about a good story that we all like, and why are these aspects so powerful? To us, it boils down to five essential components. Effective content must (1) humanize its subject matter, (2) offer distinctive value, (3) keep things simple, (4) be viral-ready, and (5) possess a transformative quality.

1: Humanize

Having the proper human appeal for your content is essential for effectively getting your message across. In an era where practically anyone can produce content, making sure that readers can connect at a basic level will help your content stand out in powerful ways. By taking the extra time to make sure that your content is human, you are demonstrating your brand's values to your community and illustrating that you aren't simply going through the motions. By doing this, you are telling the world that you think this information is valuable, and not just a task that you were forced to complete as a part of your job.

Humanizing your content means finding its emotional core, as well as how it relates to your brand's mission, vision, and values. Our emotional connections are the essence of what makes us human, and they lie at the heart of every good story. This also makes it the best litmus test for brand storytelling. If employees can't find a connection to the stories they are producing, if they can't relate it back to the fundamental vision of their personal brand, let alone their company's brand, then their customers won't be able to either. Scott Davis said it best:

> If your employee base doesn't get it, if they aren't able to give the elevator pitch, if they do not know what role they are supposed to be playing in bringing the brand to life, then they are most likely not wearing their brand on their sleeve. If this is the case, your organization is undermining its brand's full potential.

2: Be Distinctive

In the last chapter, we addressed one of the common refrains of the past 30 years: the ubiquitous claim that "everyone is a unique snow-flake." It's easy to find comfort in this idea—people do feel rather good about themselves knowing they have a distinctiveness all their own. However, being a distinct entity shouldn't be a means to an end in and of itself. Distinct content is valuable primarily because of the way it contributes to larger entities, such as brands or communities of interest. Just as Ethan McCarty illustrated with his bag of marbles metaphor (see Chapter 5), the great benefit of bringing an individual, distinct voice into the mix is the way it adds "surface area" to larger groups. Distinctive content shows that a brand isn't a one-trick pony, that it offers multiple pathways for customers or other interested parties to explore.

Being distinct and being human go hand in hand. Activate your social employees around the idea of being themselves, and they will naturally produce distinct content. Each employee has a unique set of connections to influencers, thought leaders, and customers in their extended social networks. Every different network that a social employee can leverage will produce unique results and spark their own worthwhile exchanges. Let the ideas and exchanges flow naturally, and the uniqueness will naturally follow. As our friend David Aaker, Vice-Chairman at Prophet, said:

> The key is making the content substantive and interesting so that the right people are motivated to participate. To achieve this, the topic and interaction pattern should have substance, and any interactions it produces should be evaluated and rewarded.

3: Keep It Simple

Your brand is interesting, and you have a lot you want to say about it. We get it. Just remember that the more you say all at once, the less your audience is going to retain. Social business really is about the journey, after all; consumers would rather enjoy a steady stream of small, easy-to-digest messages presented to them over the course of several days, weeks, or months than have to suffer through information overload in a single sitting.

In order to create focused, useful pieces of content for a marketing campaign, we think it's best to start with an idea tree. Begin with a high-level component of your brand story that you want to communicate to your audience. Now, break it down into smaller components by identifying three essential arguments that support your story. Repeat this process: for each of these arguments, break them down again into three more subarguments.

By taking this approach, you will have quickly outlined nine individual pieces of content all based on a single idea. Each piece can stand on its own, but taken together it establishes credibility and reinforces a larger, essential truth about a brand's story. By allowing each piece of content to revolve around a focused goal, you will have achieved a simple, easy-to-understand message. Once all the individual pieces are in place, consider ways that the information can be bundled or linked together so that users can easily navigate from item to item. In the case of blogs, for instance, making sure that each post is tagged as part of a larger category is essential for linking content.

4: Be Viral-Ready

It's no secret that going viral is every content marketer's dream. Who wouldn't want to produce a compelling piece of content that ignites online communities and compels them to share with everyone they know? The problem, of course, is that going viral is nearly impossible to do on purpose. Chipotle didn't know the kind of impact their "Back to the Start" video would have when they first put it out there, but online communities have an uncanny ability to identify and distribute the cream of the crop when it comes to online content. So, while content marketers should never attempt to design something with the explicit purpose of going viral, they should make sure that it's viral-ready.

And the best way to make sure your content is viral-ready? Once again, keep it simple. Even if a user enjoys a piece of content, they're unlikely to share it if it's a 20-minute video. If the content is less involving and easy to digest, however, the consumer will be happy to pass it along through their own networks.

Shareability also depends on the type of content your target audience is used to consuming. Do they prefer infographics or blog posts, embedded videos or podcasts? Chances are your target audience prefers more than one kind of content type, so it's good to vary your approach and presentation. Whatever the case may be, identify your audience and their media consumption habits ahead of time. By doing this, employee brand ambassadors can ensure they're speaking the same language as the audience they're trying to reach.

5: Transformation

This one isn't always the easiest thing to pin down, but here's the basic idea: your content should leave the consumer in a different place than where they began. Chipotle's "Back to the Start" video actually implies the transformation right in its name. The clip begins on a small, agrarian farm. As it progresses, the farm continues to grow, until eventually it's a large, grey factory compressing pigs into cubes and shipping them out on big semi-trucks. However, as the trucks drive off, we see a farmer have an epiphany: he decides that going "back to the start" is actually the best way to move forward. In this case, the transformation is actually a return. Only this time, what was once the familiar is made entirely new the second time around.

Transformation is that clinching moment, that little bit extra that propels good content into greatness. It's not enough just to learn something—it must compel you into action. In the age of mass media, each of us learns plenty of "somethings" every single day. Good content must do more than that. It must transform people somehow, affecting their perspectives on their communities, the products they consume, and the brands from which they buy.

Here again we urge marketers to place authenticity first. Transformation does not necessarily mean moving a customer toward a sale. In the Möbius Model we presented in Chapter 2, we demonstrated that the purchase and engagement cycle is fluid—and unending. We are all constantly moving along a shared, cyclical plane toward different outcomes. Not every outcome needs to result in a sale: often generating leadership and credibility within the community can result in even more powerful outcomes down the road.

Content Syndication Is the Key to Expand Reach

"It's hard enough to justify the budget to create the content, but it's even more challenging to then push for sufficient budget above and beyond the content creation to distribute this great content," said Greg Samarge, Digital Marketing Manager at Nestle.[7] Even viral-ready content won't distribute itself. Marketers have to be able to get content in front of the right audiences, and they must be able to do so in cost-effective ways by leveraging the voices of their communities of interest.

The secret to amplifying your social brand message is syndication. For example, in 2012, Blue Focus Marketing won the 2012 MarketingSherpa Reader's Choice Award for "Best Social Media Marketing Blog." While we hope that we won this award in part because we offered our readers valuable content and built good communities around the ideas contained within, we are certain that our advanced processes for building engaged, human distribution networks played a key role as well. We call this process the Blue Stream Content Syndication Model™. This useful approach to syndication allows marketers to reach their audiences at a very low cost.

This model is based on the idea that readers share messages as part of their daily social activities. These are in turn shared by others who also share, and so on, across additional networks. According to David Edelman at McKinsey & Company:

> *An average click-through rate for an online ad is about .03 percent. The average click-through rate when someone passes along that ad to someone else, however, is four times that number. And the reach of the ad is magnified by six times because that person passes the link along to more people.*[8]

Earned media is essential to fueling a social employee content marketing strategy, and it is precisely for this reason that marketers can't approach content marketing without a plan for both production and promotion.

The Final Frontier: Brand Choreography™

The shift from outbound to inbound marketing has brought with it some monumental changes in the process. Each of us, consumer and employee, travels social channels every day while seeking out the most useful information, more meaningful connections, and superior products. Regardless of our goals, each of us instinctively seeks out connections in order to satisfy our needs.

We are learning that brands live in these connections. If they hope to capitalize on these connections down the road, they must learn to develop a powerful content strategy, reach the right audience, and ensure that the timing of their content delivery is consistent and well-measured.

Blue Focus Marketing created a new way of thinking about the integration of marketing communications activities that we call Brand Choreography™. Essentially, this process involves the orchestration of all appropriate marketing messages and tactics—whether across traditional, digital, or social media platforms—in order to impact critical brand touch points. By following this approach, the brand supports a consumer's buying process at each step—from acquiring information and making purchases to experiencing and recommending products. As our Möbius Model indicated, the social employee plays a critical and fluid role in this connected process, navigating the digital bazaar from the brand to the customer and back.

How to Create Content to Engage Social Employees

1. **Identify a core story** in the heart of your brand's value proposition. This will fuel the creation of key messages.
2. **Develop your story platform.** Infuse it with big ideas. Those ideas must be linked to your brand value proposition and your business goals so prospects can identify with them.
3. **Map the delivery of your brand story** to your audience's information needs and buying stages.
4. **Train your social employees.** Arm them with the silver bullets (your story) that they need to impact customers in social media.
5. **Focus on communicating what you do, not what you sell.** Social media forces you to think differently. This isn't about pitching products. Engaging content works like the North Star, guiding your audience toward your brand.

6. **Develop your storylines and publish to all relevant touch points**, from blogs to Twitter and Facebook and across your brand's ecosystem. Work to create remarkable content that gets noticed and shared. The beauty of social media is the users' ability to share content they deem worthy. Basically, really good ideas have legs that extend across a myriad of touch points.

7. **Focus on creating high-value (remarkable) content** to reinforce and extend your brand, contain news value, start conversations, and engage your audience.

8. **Deliver real and unexpected benefits.** Tell the users something they didn't know so they come away smarter.

9. **Syndicate and share through every network connection available,** starting with the social employees' own network. This adds the all-important element of authenticity and builds trust between the brand, customers, and prospects.

Leveraging Content Across Multiple Platforms

In our conversations with IBM, we had the opportunity to speak with Ed Abrams, VP of Marketing–Midmarket at the company, about effective strategies for making content marketing work for any business. Now that we've discussed the underlying principles of crafting successful content, let's take a look at how IBM builds content marketing strategies in order to create the biggest impact:

> The proliferation of devices, digital media capabilities, and social media capabilities puts the customer in control of the conversation. We have data that shows that 80 percent of the time when small and medium businesses are going to make a technology decision they start their evaluation with a search engine query. So if that is where it starts, what is the right way for a company to show up in a search?
>
> For IBM, it all starts with very active listening strategies. We have actually built what we call customer intent models that allow us to look at the conversations in the marketplace and tie them back

to specific business priorities that we have. Take, for example, business analytics. We are able to identify the types of conversations that are relevant to our products and services and to our capabilities and our customer's needs. With that modeling, we are able to know the type of content that we need to deliver.

The beauty of engagement in social media and blogs is that there is now a proliferation of experts out there and expert opinions around which you can drive content. Because of this, we are looking more and more at delivering our content through our owned properties. When we look at "owned," we think not only of our digital web portal, but about the IBM midmarket Facebook and Twitter presence we have. This is where our employees and our experts become part of what we own. Our management system at this point is quite sophisticated in knowing when and how certain types of content should go out through our Facebook and Twitter handles.

This is the content that we will drive to IBM experts to tweet about, and this is the content that we will have our influencers really drive into the marketplace on our behalf. These strategies change based on the conversations happening online and the time of year, but regardless of the community needs that are driving a specific conversation, our content always has a linking strategy. For instance, our tweets point back to our Facebook page, which points back to our YouTube channel, which points back to the IBM web pages—all with the intention of helping the user to learn more information.

It all has a kind of self-selecting capability, because we start with a broad marketplace need and discussion. As the customer or prospect engages through any of those channels, we help guide them to self-select things that are more specific to IBM offerings that we bring to the marketplace.

CHAPTER 16

The Blue Focus Marketing 10 Commandments of Brand Soul

During the many interviews we conducted for this book, one idea that was continuously shared with us was the concept of DNA. This term, as we came to understand it, indicates practices and mindsets that lie at the very core of a brand's values. The elements that make up a brand's DNA come as naturally to a company as breathing, and they are just as valuable to a brand's existence.

A recent WARC article took this concept a step further by establishing the concept of a brand's "soul."[1] This idea captured our imaginations, as it sounded to us that a brand's soul would be a natural extension of its DNA. If DNA represented the essential components that make up what we are at our core, then the soul would represent what we make from those components. The soul is what happens when the raw materials of DNA meet the imagination of the social employee. The soul is a brand's values put into action to generate real-world results.

At the end, this is what we're all remembered by: that delicate balance between the things we did and our motivations for doing them. With that said, we leave you with these final thoughts, our 10 commandments for building a brand's soul.

The Blue Focus Marketing 10 Commandments of Brand Soul

1: It's All About the People

Our conversations with executives, employees, industry thought leaders, and analysts yielded several variations on one general theme: Customers do not do business with a logo. They do business with other people. It has always been true that individual contributions drive a company's destiny, but today we are coming to recognize the value of this process in new ways. Activate your employees on individual levels, empower them to take charge of their destinies within the company, and watch your brand's social currency multiply. Give employees input into your brand's mission, vision, and values. Let them see the big picture value of the work they do to show them how their contributions lead to stronger community bonds at every level.

2: The "Why" Drives Everything

The modern brand must represent the shared values of a dedicated group of individuals. Social employees don't simply want a job—they want to contribute to an organization that reflects the positive change they seek to create in the world. Social media is leading the world to new levels of global awareness, and the employees of the future will no longer accept working for organizations that fail to offer dynamic, inspiring visions of the future. The *why* directly feeds the brand's soul. It offers a reason for being that is of real social value, one that extends far beyond simple ideas of profit and commerce. Help your employees make your *why* their own, and they will reward you with nothing less than their best efforts.

3: Establish Trust Through Guardrails

A good deal of this book has been spent talking about the value of freedom for the social employee. Brands have to trust their employee brand ambassadors to represent their best interests, but that doesn't mean those employees should have carte blanche. To borrow an old aphorism, the lunatics cannot run the insane asylum. While it may sound like a contradiction to some, the truth is that, in the business sense at least, freedom only works within established boundaries. Give people unbridled freedom, and it will be hard enough for them to stay on task, let alone to accomplish specific business objectives. Guardrails or guidelines must be meant to inspire creativity, not to stifle it. If your employee tells you that the rules are standing in the way of achieving results, reconsider the rules.

4: Make Culture and Empowerment a Priority

What's the best way to drive a healthy corporate culture and empower your workforce? Give your employees a stake in it. When IBM needed a set of blogging and social media guidelines, the company put the question to its employees. Those guidelines are now considered a Magna Carta of sorts for social businesses, and have been adopted by countless other companies. If your social business wants to create a culture of contribution and empowerment, then every new task and every new decision is an opportunity to apply those values. Model your brand's values in everything you do, and watch your culture grow. Recognize and reward your social employees when they achieve desired outcomes. Nothing builds culture and empowerment quite like the feeling of being recognized for a job well done.

5: Seek Out Opportunities for Collaboration and Engagement

During the infamous Apollo 13 mission in 1970, astronauts Jim Lovell, Ken Mattingly, and Fred Haise became stranded in a disabled lunar module on their way to the moon. Faced with this crisis, the NASA crew in Houston not only had to try to get the astronauts home, but they had to make sure the astronauts could breathe. The carbon dioxide filter in the lunar module had not been designed for prolonged use by three astronauts. Unless the NASA team came up with a solution, the astronauts would suffocate before they could reenter earth's atmosphere.

At the heart of the issue was the classic "square peg in a round hole" conundrum. In theory, they had the pieces to construct a new CO_2 filter, but those pieces were incompatible. NASA technicians took shifts to find a solution, working tirelessly to repurpose materials on the craft and create an operating, jury-rigged filter. Once they had the solution, the team was then tasked with relaying the information over radio—a process demanding extreme clarity in communication.

Businesses are faced with square-peg-in-round-hole conundrums on a near-daily basis. The consequences may not be life or death as they were for the Apollo astronauts, but they can make the difference between a company thriving or merely getting by. Create the conditions for successful collaboration—whether within teams or across departments. Social employees are born collaborators capable of producing powerful results. All they need is the proper environment in which to thrive.

6: Embrace Transparency

We originally titled this commandment "be transparent," but the reality is that the further we get into the social age, the less control brands will have over whether they are transparent or not. Social employees will have a difficult time engaging their communities if they are continually forced to act in secretive or guarded ways. Whether it involves sharing information within an organization or engaging the public authentically on social platforms, opacity is the very antithesis of social business. In the social era, brands that attempt to remain opaque are often forced into transparency against their will. Empower your employees to embrace transparency, and your brand will be better able to influence the conversations surrounding its products, practices, and policies.

7: Align the Internal with the External

The rise of social media has made brand alignment more important than ever. Your employees are your brand ambassadors to the outside world. The content they produce and the conversations they engage in all reflect directly on your company and its reputation. Whatever your brand's culture is internally, they are going to carry it outside for all the world to see. For this reason, social business must be a complete process, a closed loop that continually feeds and perpetuates itself.

In Chapter 2, we presented our Möbius Strip Model to illustrate how this process produces and rewards engagement in social business. We see our model as a complement to a similar model proposed by Edelman in 2010. Where our model is focused on the underlying principles that fuel results, Edelman's model highlighted the foundational business processes that make those principles a reality. In both, a common thread links the two: the processes of social business and social employee engagement are ongoing. (see Figure 16.1)

8: Drive Disruptive Innovation

Nothing quite epitomizes the essential difference in mindset between social business and traditional command-and-control models like the concept of disruptive innovation. Disruptive thinking means being

Figure 16.1

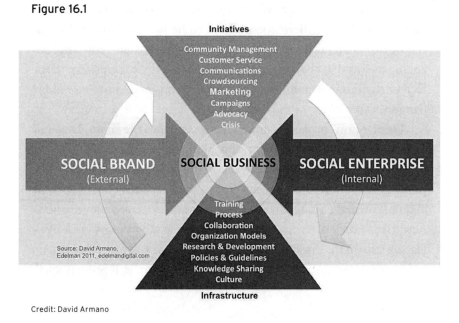

Credit: David Armano

unafraid of taking risks—even if some of those risks ultimately result in failure. In fact, champions of disruptive thinking deeply value failure, as they understand that individuals, business units, and companies at large can often stand to learn a great deal more from a misstep than they can from playing it safe all the time.

The trick to being disruptive is to carve out space for it within the organization. Planning for disruption is not the same as giving in to anarchy. As we illustrated in Chapter 11, Domo championed disruptive innovation on its quest for 100 percent social adoption within the business. Employees were shocked out of their daily routines and challenged to think differently about the way they worked, but they weren't thrown into chaos. In this example, the disruptive process came from the top, but in truth disruption can—and should—come from anywhere within the organization. Reward alternative thinking within your business, and remove the barriers that prevent your innovators from being heard.

9: The Path Is Not Predetermined

Social businesses must set long-term goals just like any other organization. Every brand must have a strong sense of where they want to be one year, five years, or even 10 years down the road. However, the pathway to getting there doesn't have to be predetermined. In fact, the rate of change that the business community is currently experiencing means that charting a course and doggedly sticking to it in the face of changing business needs is not only misguided but incredibly dangerous.

Think of this process as following a wave into the shore. Depending on where you find yourself riding along the wave, you could either wind up safely at rest along the shore or dashed against the rocks. The pathway to either outcome isn't linear, and depends entirely on the choices you make along the way. The activated social employee knows how to read the currents and adjust the course accordingly. As long as leaders within the organization have established a strong value system for its employees to follow, a safe path to the shore will present itself.

10: The Cardinal Rule: Be Human

From the moment technology became an inarguable fact of human existence, humankind has worried that as these new tools for living were adopted, humanity would be lost along the way. Even science fiction writers 100 years ago envisioned a day where all processes were automated and robots catered to our every need. In the early twenty-first century, we now have access to tools that have quite literally expanded humankind's consciousness and ability to connect. We are finding, however, that the more tools we have at our disposal to achieve monumentally complex tasks, the more important the human element becomes.

An organization's employees are its greatest resource. The social employees lie at the heart of a brand's soul. Treat them with respect and dignity. Make them feel like a human being. Seek their input with every step of the decision-making process. Empower them to represent your organization in the digital village. Give them the freedom to make choices on behalf of the brand, and as a community you will grow your brand's soul.

The Future: Coming Soon

In early 2012, we were invited to contribute to *Wharton's Advertising 2020* project as part of its "Future of Advertising" program. We were asked two questions: "What could/should advertising look like in 2020?" and "What should we do now to get ready for that future?" In considering our response, we realized that any estimation of the future must necessarily be grounded in the present. To put it another way, we can never fully understand what the future might have in store for us unless we strive to understand and embrace the environments in which we find ourselves today.

Make no mistake, the future is coming soon. As we plan for an ever brighter tomorrow, we know one thing for certain: social business is neither a fad nor a trendy buzzword cooked up to boost blogger traffic. It is both the future and the present, and at the center of it all lies the greatest difference maker of all—the social employee.

It is our duty and our pleasure as citizens of the digital village to help usher in a new era for business, an era that will continue to transform the very nature of value and engagement, of customer and brand. As your company keeps a weather eye on the horizon, we ask that you remember one thing: the practices you adopt today are the benchmarks for how you will be remembered in the future.

The journey each company begins today is its own. We are confident that the brands bold enough to let their employees chart the course will never be led astray.

AFTERWORD

Technology is neither the story nor the secret sauce behind the highest performing brands. The story lies in their people, employees who dream, champion, live, socialize, and deliver the brand to customers. They drive the brand's real value.

Smart brands today are adept at leveraging technology, the Internet, and an array of social media tools to build and enhance their customer relationships, and hence their business. Still, Cheryl and Mark Burgess would agree that the most valuable brands are the ones that tap into and answer the deep emotional needs of both their customers *and* their employees. These needs are not modern or complex; they are time-honored—really timeless—and simple: employees need to believe in and own a stake in their brand's vision. They need to participate in the brand's purpose with their minds, hearts, and souls.

Every employee of course has material and functional requirements his or her job must meet. However, when their highest-order need—deep employee engagement, or a love for the brand, if you will—is realized, then individual, organizational, and market magic happens.

While social employee branding is a new concept, the foundations and forces behind its success are not. Some companies like Southwest Airlines have been defining and delivering the best employee branding for decades. Others like GE and Dell were onto employee-centric culture and metrics before there was Facebook, LinkedIn, and Twitter. Still others like Zappos, which was built off the Internet, have powerfully reframed and implemented a basic human idea.

Before the Web, even before CRM, highly engaged employees were driving record-setting business results at Southwest. The concept of "Servant Leadership" has been around since the 1960s. Over the last four decades, Southwest has steadily taken this idea and its business to new heights. The airline, which grew out of Dallas Love Field and trades as "LUV" on the New York Stock Exchange, has turned the traditional value pyramid upside down: employees, not customers, come first; Southwest's happy, high-spirited, engaged workers (the first group) continue to produce delighted customer passengers (the second group), whose energetic loyalty results in prosperity and happiness for shareholders (the third group). Operating with a "servant's heart" is a key tenet of "The Southwest Way."[1]

In 2003, *Harvard Business Review* reported on a new brand metric that linked employee to company performance through "The Golden Rule." Fred Reichheld and Bain & Company were able to find a strong statistical correlation between customer loyalty and company profits through a simple survey methodology. Their initial hypothesis had been in part based on the Golden Rule: if companies (and their employees) treated customers right, producing delight, the brands would profit ("good profits"); brands that exploited and underserved customers for short-term gain would ultimately suffer ("bad profits"). The Golden Rule had also inspired Southwest's leadership approach.

This metric, the Net Promoter Score (NPS), is derived by asking customers how likely they would be to recommend the company to friends or colleagues according to a 0-10 scale (Promoters rate 9-10, Passives 7-8, Detractors 0-6). The goal for a brand is to maximize the number of Promoters and learn, from non-Promoters, how to improve the customer experience. As NPS results are shared within the organization, and by department, employees can be empowered and incentivized to improve the operation, their own performance, and the customer experience—the brand's bottom line.

GE, with CEO Jeff Immelt's strong sponsorship, is one of many leading global companies that ties employee performance and compensation to NPS data. Reichheld and Bain have also noted a high correlation between a brand's NPS and employee fulfillment ratings.

Apple, which is famous for eschewing management trends and market research, has implemented Net Promoter People (NPP) at its wildly successful retail stores. Apple wants employees to act directly on NPP feedback to fashion solutions that delight more customers. The objective is for employees to earn their own happiness by growing customer promoters and their role in embodying and leading the Apple brand.

CEO Michael Dell reviews NPS results quarterly with his cross-functional management team. The company has recently extended NPS inside the organization by surveying and asking all *employees* how likely they would be to recommend Dell as a place to work.

Brand employee-customer alignment metrics are an emerging area soon to be on every CEO's radar. At Movéo, we have developed a new brand gap methodology by running parallel NPS and brand attribute surveys with our clients' customers and employees to find key insights, opportunities, and gaps. We have also integrated social media actions data into a holistic brand dashboard. These metrics become effective, even transformational, when the CEO and cross-enterprise leaders participate in study design and follow-up actions—brand operationalization.

Lately, personal and collective happiness metrics have received the attention of top policy and business thinkers—adding more fuel to social employee branding efforts. Zappos has almost single-handedly created a brand happiness industry. The Amazon unit, besides selling shoes, runs happiness seminars, much like Disney trains professionals to enchant customers and colleagues. Coca-Cola has implemented employee happiness metrics around the world to support alignment with its eponymous brand positioning. Adobe tracks customer and employee happiness along with NPS.

What do Southwest, GE, Dell, Apple, Zappos, Coca-Cola, and Adobe have in common, aside from leading performance? They have each created a powerful brand vision and culture that emotionally motivates employees and answers their deepest needs, through affinity in mind, heart, and soul—forming in essence a "Brand Trinity":

▶ Brand Mind employees are attracted by the brand idea(s) and seek intellectual compatibility (Southwest's brand idea is about "Freedom").

▶ Brand Heart employees want to feel passion, see themselves in a human brand, and contribute to building something that improves lives and the world (Southwest's identity even has a heart and "LUV").

▸ Brand Soul employees yearn for higher purpose and meaning (personal and shared), want *to believe* (just ask the people of Apple or Zappos if they do), and perhaps find a spiritual connection (Southwest's brand character happens to be "Spirited").

These core, essentially human features—and concepts like Servant Leadership, the Golden Rule, and Happiness—make up the *operating systems* for the world's most valuable brands. Social employee branding strategies and tools can be powerful *applications* for enhancing brand relationships and value.

Cheryl and Mark Burgess have written an original, compelling story about the rise of social employee branding. *The Social Employee* eloquently and methodically documents what happens when brands give employees the social tools to communicate and solve problems—whether with their colleagues or with their customers, or with both at the same time. Clearly the brands that understand and serve the most fundamental human needs of their people have a head start in the social world.

Kevin Randall

Kevin Randall is Vice President of Brand Strategy & Research at Movéo Integrated Branding and a columnist for *Fast Company*. His thoughts and articles have also appeared in the *New York Times*, the *Wall Street Journal*, the *Atlantic*, *Wired*, and *Forbes*. Google has invited Kevin to speak to its employees about branding. He was named one of the #Nifty50 Top Twitter Men by Blue Focus Marketing and Webbiquity blog.

GLOSSARY

Baby Boomer: A generational group of people born roughly between the years of 1946 and 1964. Because of their age, this generation generally comprises management and executive-level positions today. (See also: Digital Immigrant, GenXer, Millennial)

Big Data: A term used to describe the unprecedented abundance of data that has arisen as a result of the digital age. Data capture techniques through websites and social platforms produce data points at such a rate that many businesses struggle to both store and process the information.

Blue Focus Marketing Möbius Model™: A nonlinear model of social engagement between employees, customers, and prospects. The Mobius strip represents a 360-degree continuum for social communication inspired by the leadership of social executives who empower employees to seek out rich social interactions for the good of the brand. (See also: Möbius Strip)

Brand: The label under which a company produces a line of products. For instance, The Coca-Cola Company produces products under brand names such as Coca-Cola, Powerade, Fanta, and Odwalla. A brand is the sum total of the entire customer experience: the collection of perceptions in the mind of the consumer.

Brand Choreography™: Involves the orchestration of all appropriate marketing messages and tactics—across traditional, digital, and social media platforms—designed to impact critical brand touch points. BC links to the consumer's basic buying process to provide solutions at each step as buyers seek to reach their goals of acquiring information, making purchases, customer experience, etc. The end result is the successful achievement of a firm's business objectives. (See also: Integrated Marketing Communications)

Brand Value Proposition (BVP): Essentially, the BVP offers customers a reason for choosing a certain brand over others. Brand value can be measured through concepts of functionality or emotional appeal, as well as through more difficult-to-measure "intangible" benefits.

Business-to-Business (B2B): Trade and communications conducted between two businesses. This term is applicable to the many businesses, especially those in the tech sector, that specialize in offering business solutions to other companies.

Business-to-Customer/Consumer (B2C): Trade and communications conducted between a business and the buying public at large. Common examples of a B2C business include companies specializing in retail and hospitality.

Change Agent: The change agent, as the name suggests, is the practical champion of change. Whereas evangelists often drive the spirit, or the *why* of a new system, product, or service, change agents work to put those new tools into practice by championing the steps necessary for an effective transition. (See also: Evangelist)

Click-Through Rate (CTR): A method for measuring the success of a specific link or ad in a marketing campaign based on the amount of clicks the link receives.

The Cloud/Cloud Computing: Cloud-based data storage and collaboration practices have grown in increasing popularity in just a few years' time. In a cloud, data is stored on a series of remote servers, allowing access to information and files. This approach reduces the chance of data being lost and enhances users' ability to share information in real time.

Command-and-Control: The most predominant management practice of the past century, the command-and-control method operates on a strict hierarchy and authority structure. While this structure benefits from each member having a clearly defined role, because decision making is highly delineated, businesses operating under this approach are not always the quickest to respond to market needs.

Content Marketing: The creation and application of all marketing content formats across relevant touch points, or a process of building brand authority and thought leadership through the production of content related to a person or brand's areas of expertise. Examples of content marketing tactics include blogs, video, white papers, infographics, etc. (See also: Curation)

Crowdsourcing: A collaborative process that utilizes the accumulated knowledge, skills, and talent base of a large group of individuals with the intention of discovering unique, innovative ideas quickly and affordably. Collaborative crowdsourcing almost always depends on a social media platform to facilitate the exchanges. This can be performed either within an organization or externally.

Curation: A form of content marketing, this process involves collecting preexisting content centered around a specific question or theme and presenting it in a valuable way. Bloggers, for instance, will often curate related content from other blogs in order to present a wide range of voices on a subject of interest.

Customer Relationship Management (CRM): This term applies to any platform or process that helps a brand organize and automate the customer engagement process. A properly designed CRM helps marketers track elements such as interactions, sales, marketing, and technical support with individual customers. CRM systems help brands ensure that prospects don't slip through the cracks or become overinundated with marketing materials.

C-Suite: A term used to refer to the group of chief executives at a company. The "C" refers to the frequent use of the word "chief" in executive job titles (e.g., chief executive officer, chief marketing officer, chief financial officer, etc.).

Digital Bazaar: Existing within the digital village, this can be seen as the social marketplace online. In other words, the digital bazaar is where business relationships are formed and deals get done. (See also: Digital Village)

Digital Immigrant: This common term is used to describe people who were born before computer use became common in homes and businesses, or who for other reasons did not grow up with regular access to computers and the Internet. Because the Internet and other computing protocols are not natural skills for digital immigrants, they require guidance in developing foundational skills. (See also: Digital Native)

Digital Native: The analog to the digital immigrant. The digital native has grown up around computers, the Internet, and social technology. The online world is a natural, integrated extension of the world at large. Training the digital native is less a question of adopting the *how* of a social/digital process, and more a question of *why*. (See also: Digital Immigrant)

Digital Village: This term is commonly used to describe online social communities and environments. Unlike in the digital bazaar, interactions in the digital village don't have to be transactional in nature. Interactions of all kind are welcome in the many different kinds of communities in the digital village. (See also: Digital Bazaar)

Disruptive Innovation: To use the common vernacular, these are game changers. Products or services that fall under the disruptive innovation umbrella effectively change the nature and needs of a particular market or way of doing things—and in many cases can create entirely new, untapped markets for exploration.

DNA: This term is used to describe the essential traits of a brand that make it unique. These traits can include a brand's mission, vision, and values, items that can then help establish a company's organizational structure and culture. (See also: Soul)

Employee Branding: The process social employees undertake in order to create a unique brand identity that reflects both the individual's authentic personality and the goals of the brand the employee represents.

Engage: This social activity serves a function both internally within a brand and externally to a brand's customers. Engagement involves the process of sharing valuable thoughts, information, content, or comments across social networks and blogs. The goal of engagement, whether internally or externally, is to produce buy-in, to activate others around a specific set of ideas, initiatives, etc.

Evangelist: The most vocal change agents for a brand. Although usually located within a company's ranks, evangelists are anyone who buys into a brand's mission, vision, and values, working tirelessly to promote those ideals and championing disruptive innovation practices in the process.

Gamification: This practice operates under the principle that people are more likely to achieve desired behaviors if this task or goal is presented as a gaming or rewards system. Rewards can include "leveling up" (earning a higher level of expertise), virtual badges, or unlocking hidden content. These processes can be used either within an organization to drive employee adoption of new practices or in public outreach programs to build brand awareness.

GenXer: This term refers to members of a demographic group born between the early 1960s and early 1980s. Because most GenXers were born either right before or during the general public adoption phase of digital technologies, they tend to be adaptive to new digital platforms and protocols. (See also: Baby Boomer, Millennial, Digital Native)

Inbound Marketing: While the term outbound marketing applies to traditional promotional tactics, inbound marketing operates on a philosophy of drawing users to web-based content though search engine optimization (SEO), email campaigns, and content marketing. Inbound marketing generally attempts to foster richer engagement through the production of dynamic, shareable content. (See also: Outbound Marketing/Push Marketing)

Integrated Marketing Communications (IMC): A communications process that involves the planning, creation, integration, and implementation of multiple forms of communications delivered to a brand's target audience. IMC attempts to result in reaching and impacting the right customers, with the right messages at the right time and place. (See also: Brand Choreography™)

Intranet: Closed systems operating under the same basic operating principles of the Internet. Many organizations use intranet systems for internal communication and information sharing to ensure that sensitive information doesn't reach the public.

Key Performance Indicator (KPI): Think of KPIs as benchmarks defined by an organization to ensure that it is on target for reaching specific goals. KPIs can be used in any aspect of any organization, whether the goal is driving culture change or rolling out a new marketing campaign.

Marketing: A process by which a firm profitably translates customer needs into revenue.

Millennial: Also sometimes referred to as "Generation Y" or the "Net Generation," millennials indicate the demographic group born between the early 1980s and early 2000s. This group is considered the first true "digital native" generation, having been born at a time where digital and computing platforms had already reached mainstream acceptance. (See also: Baby Boomer, GenXer, Digital Native)

Möbius Strip: Despite the appearance of looking like a twisted brace-let, a Möbius Strip is a nonorientable object with a single, continuous surface and only one boundary component. It can be created easily by giving a twist to a single strip of paper and then connecting the ends.

Outbound Marketing/Push Marketing: A term used to describe traditional marketing approaches, such as billboards, magazine ads, and TV commercials. Outbound marketing focuses on visibility and exposure rather than prolonged engagement or interaction.

Reverse Mentor: A growing business practice in which senior members of an organization receive coaching and support from subordinate employees. As social adoption continues to grow within business, more organizations are employing this strategy to ensure that their senior-level digital immigrants achieve a higher level of literacy in digital/social technology.

Silo: Areas in a business's organizational structure where information is either hoarded or slow to be disseminated. Because many employees still operate under the idea that information equals power, silos often form for internal political reasons. However, silos are just as likely to form because proper information sharing and distribution protocols and platforms have yet to be established.

Small-to-Medium Business (SMB): As its name implies, this term applies to businesses with approximately 500 or fewer employees. Many companies specialize in offering business solutions specifically designed for firms of this size.

Social Brand: A social brand speaks to customers (but does not shout), realizing the value of authentic, transparent engagement. It utilizes social media tools to engage with both employees and customers in order to enhance communication, accountability, and culture. A social brand bridges the relationship between the social employee and the social customer and/or prospect.

Social Communication: The term applies specifically to any kind of communication that is mediated through social platforms, whether public-facing services such as Twitter or LinkedIn or internal services such as Salesforce or Connections.

Social Currency: A term used to describe the level of respect or credibility that a brand or an individual has earned as a result of strong social engagement through social platforms.

Social Employee: A social employee is any employee who uses social philosophies—including communication, collaboration, and digital techniques—as a means of improving the business experience. This can include internal collaboration by utilizing social tools for project management and real-time communication. Externally, this can include customer engagement through public-facing social media platforms, blogging, or content marketing. The social employee fuels the social brand, working to instill humanity and authenticity in every activity they perform. (See also: Social Executive)

Social Enterprise: See Social Brand

Social Executive: These change agents empower the social employee, set the tone for the corporate culture, and ensure that employees buy in to the firm's mission, vision, and values. They recognize the value of social media in business, and operate as evangelists or change agents in order to model best practices and drive adoption. (See also: Change Agent, Evangelist, and Social Employee)

Social Listening: This process involves monitoring social media channels through specifically defined keyword searches to determine what is being said about a brand, sentiment analysis, as well as who is saying it and how much influence they have. This process is essential for any social marketing campaign, as it helps brands to better define and address their audience's needs.

Soul: In the business sense, a brand's soul can be defined as the human by-product of its DNA. If employees buy in to a brand's mission, vision, and values, they will embody those traits in all aspects of their work, building an identity and sense of purpose unique to the company. (See also: DNA)

Sticky: Sticky content or relationships produce dynamic interactions that tend to provide continuous, lasting engagement. By its very nature, sticky is not superficial.

Thought Leaders: Individuals or organizations identified as thought leaders are known innovators. They propel conversations forward and identify emerging business trends, encouraging other community members to do the same.

Touch Point: This term refers to the many different potential points of contact between a brand and its customers. Touch points can be basic considerations like a product's packaging, conversation with a customer service representative, or they can be dynamic interactions via social media channels, etc.

Viral: The term used to describe a piece of content that is rapidly distributed through online and social networks.

Wiki: Websites that are developed and modified by an open community of members who each have equal input in the site's content.

NOTES

Introduction

1. Cheryl Burgess. "The Rise of the Employee Brand." *Blue Focus Marketing*. http://www.bluefocusmarketing.com/blog/ 2012/03/01/ the-rise-of-the-employee-brand/

Chapter 1

1. Mark Fidelman. *Socialized!* (Brookline: Bibliomotion, 2012), Kindle edition: location 2891.
2. Mike Myatt. "10 Reasons Your Top Talent Will Leave You." *Forbes*. Accessed January 8, 2013. http://www.forbes.com/sites/ mikemyatt/2012/12/13/10-reasons-your-top-talent-will-leave-you/
3. Jennifer Aaker. "Building Brands Inside Out." *eCorner: Stanford University's Entrepreneurship Corner*. Accessed January 8, 2013. http:// ecorner.stanford.edu/authorMaterialInfo.html?mid=2580
4. John Hagel. "The Paradox of Preparing for Change." *Edge Perspectives with John Hagel*. Accessed November 16, 2012. http:// edgeperspectives.typepad.com/edge_perspectives/2012/10/the -paradox-of-preparing-for-change.html
5. Ibid.
6. Mark Fidelman. *Socialized!* Kindle edition: location 201.
7. Dion Hinchcliffe and Peter Kim. *Social Business by Design* (San Francisco: John Wiley & Sons, 2012), 20.
8. "Global Advertising: Consumers Trust Real Friends and Virtual Strangers the Most." *Neilsen*. Accessed November 16, 2012. http:// blog.nielsen.com/nielsenwire/consumer/global-advertising- consumers-trust-real-friends-and-virtual-strangers-the-most/
9. Don Tapscott. "Four Principles for the Open World," *TED*. Accessed November 17, 2012. http://www.ted.com/talks/don_tap_ scott_four_principles_for_the_open_world_1.html?quote=1720

Chapter 2

1. Simon Mainwaring. *We First* (New York: Palgrave Macmillan, 2012), 46. Emphasis in original.
2. Marissa Cavallos. "A New Twist on the Möbius Strip." *Science*. Accessed November 18, 2012. http://news.sciencemag.org/science- now/2007/07/16-02.html

3. Vala Afshar and Brad Martin. *The Pursuit of Social Business Excellence* (Sonoma: Charles Pinot, 2012), Kindle Edition: locations 266-268.
4. Simon Mainwaring. "Simon Mainwaring Speaker's Reel." *We First.* Accessed November 17, 2012. http://wefirstbranding.com/speaking
5. Roxane Divol, David Edelman, and Hugo Sarrazin. "Demystifying Social Media." *McKinsey Quarterly.* Accessed January 9, 2013. http://www.mckinsey.com/~/media/mckinsey/dotcom/insights/marketing%20sales/demystifying%20social%20media/demystifying%20social%20media.ashx

Chapter 3

1. Dion Hinchcliffe and Peter Kim. *Social Business by Design* (San Francisco: John Wiley & Sons, 2012), 25.
2. Simon Sinek. "How Great Leaders Inspire Action." *TED.* Accessed November 19, 2012. http://www.ted.com/talks/simon_sinek_how_great_leaders_inspire_action.html
3. David Armano. "Social Business Planning in 2012 (and Beyond)." *Edelman Digital.* Accessed October 31, 2012. http://www.edelmandigital.com/2011/12/15/social-business-planning/
4. Amy Mae-Elliot. "How the Remote Workforce Is Changing." *Mashable.* Accessed November 19, 2012. http://mashable.com/2011/10/10/remote-workforce-changing/

Chapter 4

1. "Brand Advocates Are Here to Help." *eMarketer.* Accessed November 13, 2012. http://www.emarketer.com/Article.aspx?R=1009074&ecid=a6506033675d47f881651943c21c5ed4
2. Ibid.
3. David Armano. "The Age of Brandividualism." *Experience Matters.* Accessed November 14, 2012. http://experiencematters.criticalmass.com/2009/01/23/the-age-of-brandividualism/
4. Kevin Casey. "10 Crowdsourcing Success Stories." *The Brain Yard.* Accessed November 14, 2012. http://www.informationweek.com/thebrainyard/slideshows/view/229300432/10-crowdsourcing-success-stories?pgno=1

Chapter 5

1. See Mark Fidelman, "Why Every Company Needs to Be More like IBM and Less Like Apple." *Business Insider* (http://www.businessinsider.com/why-every-company-needs-to-be-more-like-ibm-and-less-like-apple-2012-1), or Mark Fidelman, "Why IBM Represents the Future of Social Business." Business Insider (http://www.businessinsider.com/want-to-see-the-future-of-social-business-2011-7) for more information.
2. "IBM named Worldwide Marketshare Leader in Social Software for Third Consecutive Year." *IBM.* Accessed December 9, 2012. http://www-03.ibm.com/press/us/en/pressrelease/38066.wss

3. "IBM Invests $100 Million in Collaborative Innovation Ideas." *IBM*. Accessed December 9, 2012. http://www-03.ibm.com/press/us/en/pressrelease/20605.wss
4. Ethan McCarty. "Listening to the Voices of Social Business." *IBM*. Accessed April 4, 2013. http://asmarterplanet.com/blog/2013/02/listening-to-the-voices-of-social-business.html
5. Ibid.
6. Ibid.

Chapter 6
1. Amy-Mae Elliot. "4 Top Employers for Social Media Professionals." *Mashable*. Accessed October 27, 2012. http://mashable.com/2010/12/14/top-companies-social-media-professionals/
2. Ibid.
3. "Adobe Launches Ratings and Reviews for Flagship Products," *BazaarVoice*. Accessed December 11, 2012. http://www.bazaarvoice.co.uk/resources/case-studies/adobe-launches-ratings-and-reviews-flagship-products

Chapter 7
1. David Strom. "Dell Launches V2 of IdeaStorm." ReadWrite Enterprise. Accessed November 29, 2012. http://readwrite.com/2012/03/26/dell-launches-v2-of-ideastorm

Chapter 8
1. Cisco. *Cisco Overview*. http://newsroom.cisco.com/overview Accessed November 2, 2012.

Chapter 9
1. Christi McNeill. "Social Media Guidelines." *Nuts About Southwest*. Accessed December 11, 2012. http://www.blogsouthwest.com/files/socialmedia_guidelines2010_final.pdf
2. Christi McNeill. "Not So Silent Bob." *Nuts About Southwest*. Accessed December 11, 2012. http://www.blogsouthwest.com/blog/not-so-silent-bob
3. Stephen Dickey, "Holly, the 'Most Remarkably Kind Flight Attendant.'" *Nuts About Southwest*. Accessed December 11, 2012. http://www.blogsouthwest.com/blog/holly-most-remarkably-kind-flight-attendant
4. "Operational Impact of Sandy." *Southwest Media*. Accessed November 30, 2012. http://swamedia.com/releases/7c88130a-7106-4fd9-b61c-5d1b8af8001b?search=hurricane+sandy
5. "New Orleans Fire Fighters Return the Favor to New York City by Aiding in the Aftermath of Hurricane Sandy." *Southwest Media*. Accessed November 30, 2012. http://

swamedia.com/releases/02f1d715-9ec4-485b-8081-554ef38d8db7
?search=hurricane+sandy

6. "Hurricane Sandy Animals Flown to Safe Haven on Southwest
   Airlines Charter." *Southwest Media*. Accessed November 30, 2012.
   http://swamedia.com/releases/abd5e583-64db-44d3-96ef
   -69bbc245a743?search=hurricane+sandy

Chapter 10

1. Cheryl Burgess. "The Rise of the Employee Brand." *Blue Focus
   Marketing*. http://www.bluefocusmarketing.com/blog/2012/03/01/
   the-rise-of-the-employee-brand/

Chapter 11

1. Josh James "Let the Games Begin! Welcome to the
   #Domosocial Experiment." *Domo*. Accessed November 30,
   2012. http://www.domo.com/social/2012/05/08/let-the
   -games-begin-welcome-to-the-domosocial-experiment/
2. Ibid.

Chapter 12

1. Kimberly A. Whitler. "Why CMOs Avoid Social Media." *CMO.com*.
   Accessed December 13, 2012. http://www.cmo.com/content/cmo
   -com/home/articles/2012/10/18/why-cmos-avoid-social-media.html
2. Mark Fidelman. "Meet the Top 20 Most Social CMOs
   on Twitter." *Forbes*. Accessed December 13, 2012. http://
   www.forbes.com/sites/markfidelman/2012/11/29/
   the-top-20-social-cmos-of-the-fortune-100-visuals/
3. Steve Olenski. "When It Comes to Social CEOs, One Group
   Is the Clear Winner." *Forbes*. Accessed December 29, 2012. http://
   www.forbes.com/sites/marketshare/2012/12/18/when-it-comes-to
   -social-ceos-one-group-is-the-clear-winner/
4. Whitler. "Why CMOs Avoid Social Media."
5. David Edelman. "Social Media in the C-Suite." *Forbes*.
   Accessed December 29, 2012. http://www.forbes.com/sites/
   mckinsey/2012/03/22/social-media-in-the-c-suite/
6. Mark Fidelman. "The 7 Personality Types of Extremely Anti-Social
   Business Executives." *Forbes*. Accessed December 18, 2012. http://
   www.forbes.com/sites/markfidelman/2012/04/17/the-7-personality-
   types-of-extremely-anti-social-business-executives/
7. Cheryl Burgess. "7 Personalities of a Social Executive." *Blue Focus
   Marketing*. Accessed December 18, 2012. http://www.bluefocusmar-
   keting.com/blog/2012/05/16/7-personalities-of-a-social-executive/
8. Paul Hagen. "The Rise of the Chief Customer Officer." *Forbes*.
   Accessed December 19, 2012. http://www.forbes.com/2011/02/10/
   chief-customer-officer-leadership-cmo-network-rise.html

9. Dion Hinchcliffe. "Is It Time for a C-Level Social Media Executive?" *ZDnet*. Accessed December 19, 2012. http://www.zdnet.com/blog/hinchcliffe/is-it-time-for-a-c-level-social-media-executive/2055

10. Ibid.

Chapter 13

1. "2012 World Population Data Sheet." *Population Reference Bureau*. Accessed December 28, 2012. http://www.prb.org/Publications/Datasheets/2012/world-population-data-sheet/data-sheet.aspx

2. Don Tapscott in Jacob Morgan. *The Collaborative Organization* (New York: McGraw-Hill, 2012), 276.

3. Alex Williams. "Saying No to College." The *New York Times*. Accessed December 27, 2012. http://www.nytimes.com/2012/12/02/fashion/saying-no-to-college.html

Chapter 14

1. Allex. "The Best Social Media Definition to Date." *CenterNetworks*. Accessed January 3, 2013. http://www.centernetworks.com/social-media-definition/

2. See: http://www.slideshare.net/ejoachimsthaler/vivaldi-partners-group-social-currency-2012-final-sept18

3. Examples of these and other initiatives can be found at http://www.vivaldipartners.com/vpsocialcurrency/brand/BestBuy

4. Charlene Li. "Big Idea 2013: Get All of Your Employees on Social Media." *LinkedIn*. Accessed December 28, 2012. http://www.linkedin.com/today/post/article/20121211105953-33767-big-idea-2013-get-all-of-your-employees-on-social-media

5. Ann Charles. "Can Best Buy Get Its Groove Back Through Social Media Leadership?" *Forbes*. Accessed December 22, 2012. http://www.forbes.com/sites/realspin/2012/08/14/can-best-buy-get-its-groove-back-through-social-media-leadership/

Chapter 15

1. Giselle Abramovich. "Chevy's Shift from Selling to Telling." *Digiday*. Accessed December 20, 2013. http://www.digiday.com/brands/chevys-shift-from-selling-to-telling/

2. Karen Cheung-Larivee. "Fierce Q&A: Cleveland Clinic CEO Dishes on His Expansion Goals." *Fierce Healthcare*. Accessed December 20, 2012. http://www.fiercehealthcare.com/story/fierce-qa-cleveland-clinic-ceo-dishes-expansion-goals/2012-04-26

3. Melinda Partin. "Brand Storytelling: Connecting with Your Audience." *FastCompany*. Accessed December 21, 2012. http://www.fastcompany.com/1315306/brand-storytelling-connecting-your-audience

4. Chipotle. "Back to the Start." *YouTube*. Accessed December 21, 2012. http://www.youtube.com/watch?v=aMfSGt6rHos
5. Simon Mainwaring. "How to Use Social Media to Build Your Brand Reputation, Profits, & Social Impact." *WeFirst*. Accessed December 21, 2012. http://socialbrandingblueprint.com/newmarketplace/
6. Andy Smith. "Chipotle: Food with Integrity." *The Dragonfly Effect*. Accessed January 4, 2013. http://community.dragonflyeffect.com/profiles/blogs/chipotle-food-with -integrity?xg_source=activity
7. Giselle Abramovich. "Why Brands Struggle with Content Creation." *Digiday*. Accessed December 21, 2012. http://www.digiday.com/brands/why-brands-struggle-withcontent -creation/
8. David Edelman. "Thinking Brand with Google: Winning the Customer Decision Journey." *Chief Marketing & Sales Officer Forum*. Accessed December 21, 2012. http://cmsoforum.mckinsey.com/customer-decision-journey/cmo-summit-driving-customer-focused-growth

Chapter 16

1. WARC Staff. "Brand 'Soul' Key for PepsiCo." *WARC*. Accessed January 4, 2013. http://www.warc.com/LatestNews/News/Brand_soul_key_for_PepsiCo.news?ID=30687

Afterword

1. Southwest Airlines. "Our Culture." Accessed April 8, 2012: http://www.southwest.com/html/about-southwest/careers/culture.html

ACKNOWLEDGMENTS

In writing a book that focuses quite a bit on the idea of building rich communities, we could not be more grateful to the members of our own networks. Without their stories, support, advice, contributions, and guidance, this book would have turned out very differently.

At Adobe, we'd like to thank Ann Lewnes, Maria Poveromo, Pooja Prasad, Katie Juran, and Lisa Smith for taking the time and care to make their brand's story really sizzle. A special thank you also goes out to Brad Rencher, who helped plug us in to the amazing Adobe team.

Our sincerest thanks go out to Tim Suther and Mark Zembal for bringing Acxiom's story together. Our thanks go as well to Mark Donatelli, Allison Nicholas, and Mark Ogne for contributing their own experiences to the Acxiom story.

Alicia Dietsch, Bill Strawderman, and Gina Welker at AT&T were instrumental in championing their brand's story, and we are eternally grateful for their kindness. Special thanks to the people who inspired us at AT&T: Cathy Martine, Beth Asaro, Ken Fenoglio, Shay Strode, Monica Liming-Hu, and Jim Boxmeyer. A very special thank you to Trish Nettleship, Sam Sova, and Terry Brock.

At Cisco, we would like to thank Ron Ricci and Jeremy Hartman for giving us such a rich look into the company's social adoption process and for teaching us the value of the *why*. We would also like to extend a special thank you to Meghan M. Biro both for her contribution to this book and for putting us in contact with Cisco.

We are very grateful to the many members of the Dell team who stepped up to help tell their brand's story. Thank you to Cory Edwards, Liz Brown, Sean Gibson, Jessica Nielsen, Amanda Burke, and John Boyle for all your hard work in making this chapter come to life. Also, a very special thank you to Michael Dell.

Thank you to the pioneers at Domo, Josh James and Julie Kehoe, for telling us your wonderful story. We look forward to watching Domo continue to blaze new trails in the business world.

We cannot overstate how grateful we are for the warm welcome we received from the employees at IBM. Thank you very much to John Kennedy, Ben Edwards, Ed Abrams, Ethan McCarty, John Rooney, Sandy Carter, Suzanne Livingston, Kelly Meade, Sandra Marcus, Michelle Ulrich, and Jennifer Dubow. We would also like to extend a heartfelt thank you to Laurie Friedman, who worked tirelessly to coordinate the entire process. You truly embody what it means to be an IBMer.

At Southwest Airlines, which was a social brand before there was a term for it, our appreciation goes out to Dana Williams, Christi McNeil, Todd Painter, Linda Rutherford, Richard Matthews, and Stephen Keller. Thanks for leading the way for the rest of us.

We are also indebted to the many others who contributed content. Thank you to Simon Mainwaring, Andreas Ramos, Mark Fidelman, Tom Pick, Dion Hinchcliffe, Ann Charles, Jon Ferrara, Scott Davis, David Aaker, Jennifer Aaker, Andy Smith, Erich Joachimsthaler, David Armano, Vala Afshar, Fred Burt, Kent Huffman, Michael Brenner, Dino Dogan, Dan Cristo, Nancy Costopulos, Eric Greenberg, David Finegold, and Alex Romanovich.

To our many friends in the community who helped us with introductions, advice, and support, we couldn't have done this without you. Thank you to Mari Smith, Tom Peters, Gary Schirr, Adam Cohen, Ethne Swartz, Caroline Munoz, Deirdre Letson, Clara Nelson, Marie Parker, Anthony Yacullo, Kathy Oswald, Kevin Lane Keller, Liselotte Hägertz Engstam, Brian Solis, Dan Schawbel, Jez Frampton, Caitlyn Irwin, Kristen Daukas, Trisha Dionne, Judy Bellem, William Arruda, Ann Handley, Dave Kerpen, Peter Methot, Morgan Wells, Dennis Urbaniak, John Hagel, Gail Nelson, Chris Burgess, Jeff Bullas, Gini Dietrich, Howie Goldfarb, Jacob Morgan, Esta H. Singer, Angela Maiers, Rebel Brown, Ric Dragon, Chuck Martin, Marjorie Clayman, Billy Mitchell, BJ Emerson, Robert Rose, Lisa Petrilli, John Nosta, Tom Richardson, Eric Fletcher, Epi Ludvik Nekaj, Alan See, Steve Cassady, Mary Lou Roberts, Randy Ryerson, Susan Avello,

Catharine Findiesen Hays, Jerry (Yoram) Wind, Deborah Weinstein, Deirdre Breakenridge, Susan Mazza, Lori Moreno, Jenna Dobkin, Deborah Silver, Daniel Burstein, Steve Olenski, Shelly Kramer, Sam Fiorella, Amy Howell, Anne Deeter Gallaher, Elizabeth Hitchcock, Glen Gilmore, Stan Phelps, Mike Johansson, Peg Fitzpatrick, Paul Biedermann, Ted Rubin, Julia Gometz, Carrie Bugbee, Andrew Grill, Daniel Newman, Patrick Adams, Ann Tran, Larry Tolpin, Ted Coine, Sean Gardner, Wendy Marx, Jamie Crager, Judy Martin, Jeff Ashcroft, Scott Goodson, Cynthia and Larry Newman, Patricia Wilson, Margaret Malloy, Susan Young, Lori Ruff, Mike O'Neil, Shawn Murphy, Brian Slattery, Frank Strong, Jure Klepic, Joe and Karen Seickel, and Margaret Langsett.

Special thanks go out to David Edelman at McKinsey, a true digital visionary, for providing us with your great insights and powerful foreword. Special thanks go out as well to Kevin Randall for your inspiration, collaboration, and riveting afterword.

We of course cannot forget to thank our publisher, McGraw-Hill, for making this whole thing possible. Many thanks to Casie Vogel for her continued enthusiasm and encouragement while guiding us through the editorial maze, Pattie Amoroso for her meticulous attention to detail, Rhonda Oliver, our fantastic copyeditor, and Donya Dickerson for her vision. And a very special thank you to Andreas Ramos for your contribution, counsel, and introduction to Roger Stewart at McGraw-Hill.

We are also grateful to our contributors on the Blue Focus Marketing team. Thank you to our research assistant Chas Hoppe for your orchestration of big data, our amazing three interns, John Vassos, Shea Cuddihy, and Dylan Hoffmann, Sam Kennedy for your friendship and excellent web development work, and David Brier and Mauricio Olivera for the outstanding graphics you provided us.

Our heartfelt thanks to Norma Keith, Cheryl's mother, for her endless support and encouragement. She always wanted me to write a book, and she finally got her wish! Thanks as well to our son, Kent. How else can we say it? You're amazing and we love you very much.

Thanks to several outstanding educational institutions: Rutgers University, The Wharton School of the University of Pennsylvania, Rider University, Fairleigh Dickinson University, Centenary College, and special thanks to the American Marketing Association (AMA).

Finally, thanks to all the other members of our communities online and in the business and marketing world. You all helped make this book possible with your daily wisdom and support.

INDEX

ABOUT THE AUTHORS

Photo: Joanie Schwarz

Cheryl Burgess, cofounder, CEO, and CMO of Blue Focus Marketing, is an award-winning social branding marketer and speaker with expertise in B2B marketing. Burgess, who *Huffington Post* called a social media "Passionista," appears regularly as an expert blogger for AT&T Business Solutions. Blue Focus Marketing won the 2012 Reader's Choice Award for Best Social Media Marketing Blog. She is a member of the Wharton Advertising 2020 Contributor Community and a featured blogger at CMO.com. She is also the winner of four Twitter Shorty Awards. In 2011, she cofounded the #Nifty50 Top Men & Women on Twitter Awards. Follow her on Twitter at @ckburgess, @SocialEmployee, and @BlueFocus.

Photo: Joanie Schwarz

Mark Burgess is cofounder and president of Blue Focus Marketing, a social branding firm that helps businesses realize the power of the social employee. The firm also focuses on integrated marketing and content marketing solutions. Burgess is a digital marketer, content marketing strategist, speaker, and marketing executive. His career spans advertising, marketing, professional services consulting, and education. Mark is an expert blogger for AT&T Business Solutions. He is a member of the Wharton Advertising 2020 Contributor Community. Burgess has held senior level B2B and B2C positions at McCann, PwC, and AT&T. An adjunct MBA professor at leading universities, Burgess ranks in the Top 100 Marketing Professors on Twitter. Follow him on Twitter at @mnburgess, @SocialEmployee, and @BlueFocus.

Their website is www.bluefocusmarketing.com